Reforming Marriage

REFORMING MARRIAGE

DOUGLAS WILSON

MOSCOW, IDAHO

Douglas J. Wilson, *Reforming Marriage*

© 1995 by Douglas J. Wilson.
Published by Canon Press, P.O. Box 8741, Moscow, ID 83843
800-488-2034

01 00 99 98   9 8 7 6

Cover design by Paige Atwood Design, Moscow, ID

Printed in the United States of America.

Unless otherwise indicated, Scripture quotations are from the New King James Version of the Bible, ©1979, 1980, 1982, 1984, 1988 by Thomas Nelson, Inc., Nashville, Tennessee

ISBN: 1-885767-34-X

Of course, this book is for Nancy.
Foedus amorum est.

Reforming Marriage

Table of Contents

Introduction 9

1. A Practical Theology of Marriage 13

2. Headship and Authority 23

3. Duties of Husbands and Wives 43

4. Efficacious Love 53

5. Keeping Short Accounts 67

6. Miscellaneous Temptations 77

7. The Marriage Bed is Honorable 99

8. Multiplying Fruitfully 119

9. Divorce and Remarriage 131

Epilogue 141

Introduction

And walk in love, as Christ also has loved us and given Himself for us, an offering and a sacrifice to God for a sweet-smelling aroma (Ephesians 5:2).

How would you describe the spiritual aroma of your home? When visitors arrive, before virtually anything is said or done, what is one of the first things they notice about your family? In many cases, it is the *aroma*. Do they feel as though a bad attitude crawled under your refrigerator and died? Or do they think someone has been baking spiritual bread in the kitchen all afternoon?

Perhaps the one living in the home is not in the best position to answer this question. Aromas are the sorts of things one gets used to. The residents usually do not notice those things that immediately strike a visitor. So if there is an offensive aroma in the home, it can sometimes be a difficult problem to solve. No easy formula of resolution is available. Nevertheless, the Bible does teach on the subject. The text noted above says that when Christians walk in love they are imitating Christ, and the sacrifice of Christ is a pleasant aroma to God. Similarly, a Christ-like home atmosphere produces this sort of aroma before God and consequently before man.

In other words, keeping God's law with a whole heart (which is really what love *is*) is not only seen in overt acts of obedience. The collateral effect of obedience is the aroma of love. This aroma is out of reach for those who have a hypocritical desire to be known by others as a keeper of God's law. Many can fake an attempt at keeping God's standards in some external way. What we *cannot* fake is the resulting, distinctive aroma of pleasure to God.

In the home, where should this wholehearted obedience begin? Where should the aroma originate? Jesus taught us, with regard to individuals, that cups must be cleaned from the inside out. If we apply this principle to the home, we should see that the "inside" of a family is, of course, the relationship between husband and wife, as they self-consciously imitate the relationship of Christ and the church. John Bunyan once exhorted husbands to be "such a believing husband to your believing wife that she may say, 'God has not only given me a husband, but such a husband as preaches to me every day the way of Christ to His church.'" The health of all other relationships in the home depends upon the health of *this* relationship, and the key is found in how the husband is treating his wife. Or, put another way, when mamma ain't happy, ain't nobody happy.

Later in the fifth chapter of Ephesians, Paul tells husbands to love their wives as they love their own bodies. He then points out that each person nourishes and cherishes his own body. The word for *cherishes* in that passage literally means *to keep warm*. Consequently, one of the fundamental duties of husbandry is for the husband to keep his wife *warm*. When that is done, the rest of the home is warm. But how can he keep her warm? Notice that our text says that we are to *walk* in love. A wife is not kept warm in the securing love of a husband if he is erratic in how he loves her. If he is harsh with her or ignores her but occasionally shows her kindness, he is not walking in love. The kind of love Paul requires here is *constant*. So godly husbandry is constant husbandry.

And as the context makes clear, the love in this passage is also *imitative*. It is learned from a Person; it is learned through watching Jesus Christ. As children learn from their parents through watching them, so Christians are to learn from Christ. This means that a husband who loves his wife is *not* a pioneer. It has all been done before. Christ has loved the Church in the same the way He wants men to love their wives. He has done so as an *example*. The love and affection of Christ has been set upon His people alone. In the same way, husbands are to love their wives alone. This is the duty I hope to explain in this book in some detail.

But we should already know from all of this that such obedience is not exhausted by the external conformity to God's requirements. Godly obedience will always bring in its train a host of *intangibles*. These intangibles are what constitute the aroma of obedience, and this aspect of true obedience frustrates the paint-by-numbers approach to marriage enhancement. This is why I am afraid that this book will be of little use to those who simply want a "formula" to follow that will build them a happy marriage. When it comes to the externals, the mere copyist can always say of himself what the unregenerate Saul could say, "concerning the righteousness which is in the law, blameless." However hard the externalist tries, he cannot produce the aroma of godliness. This is why so many people attend marriage seminars and read marriage books with so little result. The obedience of the Christian man is not limited to new *actions*—actions which, after all, can be copied mechanically. This does not appear to be a rare or unusual error; many people who are miserable in their marriages are also those who have read all the books.

Of course certain actions, godly obedience in externals, must be present in all healthy marriages; but in order to produce this distinctive aroma, the externals must proceed from new *hearts*. As William Tyndale put it, when God "buildeth he casteth all downe first. He is no patcher." In the same way, the love of the Christian husband does not proceed from reading the "right books," including this one, or going to the right seminars. God will not patch His grace onto some humanistic psychological nonsense—even if that nonsense is couched and buried in Christian terminology.

It proceeds from an obedient heart, and the greatest desire of an obedient heart is the glory of God, *not* the happiness of the household. If we might paraphrase the words of the catechism, the chief end of *marriage* is to glorify God and enjoy Him forever. The reason we are miserable in our marriages is because we have idolized them. But the glory of God is more important than our domestic happiness.

In the world God made, if a creature worships anything other than the Creator God, then ultimately he loses the very thing he idolizes and worships. Husbands must love their wives; they must *not* worship them. Those who lose their lives find it, and those who seek to find it will lose it. Those who place their wives before God will lose their wives. Those who glorify God will of course obey Him in their self-sacrificial love for their wives. It should go without saying that a wife is greatly blessed when her husband loves Christ more than he loves her. When a husband seeks to glorify God in his home, he will be equipped to love his wife as he is commanded. And if he loves his wife as commanded, the aroma of his home will be pleasant indeed.

CHAPTER ONE

A Practical Theology of Marriage

Foundations

A short walk through the marriage and family section of the local Christian bookstore easily demonstrates that modern Christians have a tremendous interest in the subject of marriage and family. But this booming marriage business (books, conferences, seminars, marriage counseling) is really a sign of disease and not health. In a very real sense, our interest is morbid, almost pathological. We are like a terminal cancer patient, fervently researching alternative treatments, hoping against hope that something can be done. Desperate for happiness in our relationships, and discontent with what God has given us, we are imploring the experts to show us the way out.

God is the Lord. He is central to the coherence of all things, including marriage. He has the preeminence over heaven and earth, and all His human creatures have the moral responsibility to acknowledge that preeminence in all they do, including how they marry. A man and a woman who have this orientation together, in a covenant bond, enjoy a Christian marriage. If they deny or ignore this truth, they do so at their peril. A mature Christian is one who understands that it is the duty of all human creatures to glorify God in all things. It therefore stands to reason that a mature Christian man will be a mature husband. Likewise, a mature Christian woman will be a mature wife. *Maturity in the Lord is a prerequisite to maturity in marriage.*

In studying the subject of marriage, we must begin with the biblical instruction on the nature and character of God. When we have come to understand that He is indeed the Lord, we will naturally turn to Him to learn how His gracious law applies to the foundation and purpose of marriage.

The Covenant

The nature of the triune God is described to us in Scripture under the figure of a father-son bond. God is the *Father*, and Jesus Christ is His only *Son*. Before He laid the foundation of the earth, the Father had already selected a *bride* for His Son. That bride is the Christian church, the elect of God. "Then one of the seven angels . . . came to me and talked with me, saying, 'Come, I will show you the bride, the Lamb's wife.' And he carried me away in the Spirit to a great and high mountain, and showed me the great city, the holy Jerusalem, descending out of heaven from God" (Rev. 21:9–10).

Paul teaches us that we ought self-consciously to think of our marriages as dim pictures of the central marriage, that of Christ to His church. It is a great mystery, he says, but when a man leaves his father and mother, and takes a wife, he makes a proclamation concerning Christ and the church. Depending on the marriage, that declaration is made poorly or well, but it is always made.

We can, therefore, see how the foundation of marriage is *covenantal*. God's relationship to us through Christ is covenantal—it is the New Covenant—and our marriages are a picture of that truth. The foundation of godly married life is the same foundation for all godly living—in everything we are to seek the glory of God. Our triune God is a covenant-making and covenant-keeping God, and He has chosen *marriage* as one of the best instruments through which fallen men may glorify Him.

In attacking the covenantal nature of marriage, the error of feminism has been very valuable. Throughout the history of the church, destructive heresies have been used by a sovereign God to force the church to define that which was unclear. It was the heretic Marcion who provoked the church into identifying the canon of Scripture, the heretic Arius who forced the church to testify clearly to the full deity of the Lord Jesus, and so on. In our day, feminism is providing that same service through its challenge of the marriage covenant.

Without the defiance of error, we can very easily just drift along, doing what seems "natural" or "traditional." Countless thousands do quite a number of things because it "just seems right." When and if that practice is ever challenged, however, the traditionalist is nonplussed. "Well, I'm not sure *why* I do that, really." Consider our practice of a woman taking her husband's last name. Why do we do that? Why does Susan Miller become Susan Carter? Does the Bible require it?

Surprisingly for some, the Bible does teach that God calls a husband and wife by the same name—the name of the husband. This fully supports both our particular custom of taking a new name, as well as the covenantal truth that custom represents.

"This is the book of the genealogy of Adam. In the day that God created man, He made him in the likeness of God. He created them male and female, and blessed them and called them *mankind* in the day they were created" (Gen. 5:1). In Hebrew, the italicized word translated *mankind* is *Adam*. In other words, God created Adam and his wife male and female, He blessed them and called *them* Adam. She was, from the beginning, a covenantal partaker in the name of her husband. God does not call her Adam on her own, He calls her Adam *with him*.

Adam first noticed the lack of a suitable helper after naming the animals. "So Adam gave names to all cattle, to the birds of the air, and to every beast of the field. But for Adam there was not found a helper comparable to him. And the Lord God caused a deep sleep to fall on Adam, and he slept; and He took one of his ribs, and closed up the flesh in its place" (Gen. 2:20–21). When Adam was naming the animals, he was not just attaching labels randomly. In the ancient world, names were extremely significant and represented the nature and character of that which was named. This significance is very clear in the Genesis accounts of the naming of Adam's wife. In naming the animals, Adam saw none who could be appropriately named as a helper suitable for him.

After the creation of his wife, Adam receives her, and *names* her. "And Adam said: 'This is now bone of my bones and flesh of my flesh; she shall be called Woman [*Ishshah*, not Eve], because she was taken out of Man.' Therefore a man shall leave his father and mother and be joined to his wife, and they shall become one flesh" (Gen 2:23–24).

As verse 24 shows, Adam and Ishshah were a paradigmatic couple. *They were not just any two individuals.* When the Lord Jesus taught on the subject of divorce, He appealed to the creation ordinance of marriage found in the early chapters of Genesis. He taught us that *God* puts a man and woman together in marriage, and what God has joined together man has no authority to separate. The temptation is to argue that in Genesis God only joined together Adam and Eve—two individuals as individuals. But this argument resists the teaching of Christ, who insisted that Adam and Eve were a paradigmatic couple. When God joined *them* together, He was joining together *every* man and woman who has ever come together sexually in a covenant bond.

Other facts are obvious as well from this creation ordinance of marriage. Because God created Adam and Eve, homosexuality is excluded. Because Adam could find no helper for himself among the animals, bestiality is excluded. And because God created just *one* woman for Adam, the pattern of monogamy is clearly set and displayed to us. The polygamy found in the Old Testament among the saints of God does not alter this. Polygamy was instituted by *man*, and not by God. The first record of a polygamous union was Lamech (Gen. 4:19), with no hint of divine approval. But most important, polygamy does not fit with the creation ordinance of marriage or with the picture given in the New Testament of Christ and the church.

So in this passage of Genesis, we are taught that Adam's reception of the woman, and his naming of her, were to be a pattern for all marriages to come. "*Therefore* a man shall leave his father and mother . . ." Now at this point Adam had not yet named his wife *Eve*. Adam gave his wife two individual names. The first was Ishshah, or Woman, because she was taken out of man. The second was Chavvah—life-bearer, or as we say it in English, *Eve*. "And Adam called his wife's name Eve [*Chavvah*], because she was the mother of all living" (Gen. 3:20).

In both passages where she is named, it is clearly stated that her two names reveal truth about her. The first reveals her dependence upon man—she was taken out of man. The second reveals man's dependence upon her—every man since is her son. Millennia later, the apostle Paul teaches us that we are continually to remember these two truths in our marriages. Each wife is an *Ishshah*, and each wife is a *Chavvah*. Each is Woman, and each is Eve.

"Nevertheless, neither is man independent of woman, nor woman independent of man, in the Lord. For as woman came from man, even so man also comes through woman; but all things are from God" (1 Cor. 11:11–12). Notice that the progression of Paul's thought follows the same pattern seen in Genesis. Woman "came from man (*Ishshah*), even so man also comes through woman (*Chavvah*); but all things are from God" (*Adam*).

God is the one who called our first parents by the collective name Adam. Now Adam is also a generic term for *man* or *mankind*. This shows clearly the biblical practice of including women under such a description. Our English use of the generic *man* and *mankind* follows this biblical example exactly. Far from being insulting to women, as feminists want to maintain, it reflects a biblical pattern of thought. The feminist reaction to this, and their rejection of taking a new last name (in order to keep their *father's* name!), is not just a small bit of modern silliness. It is a fundamental rebellion against God. So when our Susan Miller becomes Mrs. Robert Carter it is not just "something we do." It is covenant security.

With this basic framework for understanding the marriage covenant, we may turn to consider the basic purposes of marriage. The Bible sets forth three basic *earthly* reasons for marriage. They are, in turn, the need for helpful companionship, the need for godly offspring, and the avoidance of sexual immorality.

Helpful Companionship

The Bible teaches that God placed Adam in the garden and gave him a task to perform. But the man was incapable of accomplishing that task alone. Adam needed help, and the woman was created to meet his need.

> Out of the ground the Lord God formed every beast of the field and every bird of the air, and brought them to Adam to see what he would call them. And whatever Adam called each living creature, that was its name. So Adam gave names to all cattle, to the birds of the air, and to every beast of the field. But for Adam there was not found a helper comparable to him. And the Lord God caused a deep sleep to fall on Adam, and he slept; and He took one of his ribs, and closed up the flesh in its place. Then the rib which the Lord God had taken from man He made into a woman, and He brought her to the man. And Adam said, "This is now bone of my bones, and flesh of my flesh; she shall be called Woman, because she was taken out of Man." Therefore a man shall leave his father and mother and be joined to his wife, and they shall become one flesh (Gen. 2:19–24).

We should be able to see the connection between Adam's work of naming the beasts and the next phrase—"but for Adam there was not found a helper comparable to him." The modern mentality tends to think of "naming things" as a simple scientific matter of attaching labels. But here Adam is naming the beasts with a name suitable to the nature of each. As mentioned above, in the process of naming, he realizes he has found no suitable helper—no one among the animals with a nature comparable to his. He could not name any as a helper.

In the verse immediately prior to this passage God had said that it was *not good* that man should be *alone*. Throughout the process of creation, whenever God completed a work, He then pronounced it good. Obviously, such a pronouncement from the Creator indicates completion. But the Lord's statement that it was not good that man be alone is a clear indication that the creation of man was still incomplete. "And the Lord God said, 'It is not good that man should be alone; I will make him a helper comparable to him'" (Gen. 2:18). Adam was incomplete because he lacked a companion, one who would be a helper comparable to him.

The New Testament applies this truth in a very interesting way. "Nor was man created for the woman, but woman for the man" (1 Cor. 11:9). As a result of the creation order, men and women are oriented to one another differently. They need one another, but they need one another *differently*. The man needs *the* help; the woman needs *to* help. Marriage was created by God to provide companionship in the labor of dominion. The cultural mandate, the requirement to fill and subdue the earth, is still in force, and a husband cannot fulfill this portion of the task in isolation. He needs a companion suitable for him in the work to which God has called him. He is called to the work and must receive help from her. She is called to the work through ministering to him. He is oriented to the task, and she is oriented to him.

Godly Children

One of the things which man obviously cannot do alone is reproduce, and this is a second purpose for marriage. In filling the earth, which is what God commanded, a man alone is completely helpless. So the prophet Malachi tells us that another stated purpose of marriage is the blessing of godly offspring.

> But did he not make them one, having a remnant of the Spirit? And why one? He seeks godly offspring. Therefore take heed to your spirit, and let none deal treacherously with the wife of his youth (Mal. 2:15).

God tells us quite plainly here that one of the purposes of marriage is procreation. Further, if it is a godly marriage, it should be godly procreation. God has said that He wants *godly* offspring. The prophet Malachi states, as a means to that end, the importance of *treating wives with honor*. If a man is treacherous to his wife, it will clearly have a negative effect on the children. Godly children are not said to give purpose to *parenting*, but rather they are a purpose of *marriage*.

Sexual Protection

Adam needed a helpful companion before the Fall. He was also unable to multiply descendants alone before the Fall. So the first two purposes of marriages mentioned above are not necessarily related to the presence of sin. But the third reason why Christians should marry is connected to the presence of sin and temptation. The apostle Paul states it this way:

> Nevertheless, because of sexual immorality, let each man have his own wife, and let each woman have her own husband. Let the husband render to his wife the affection due her, and likewise also the wife to her husband (1 Cor. 7:2–3).

We live in a fallen world, and, as a consequence, Christians frequently struggle with temptations to lust, fornication, and adultery. The Bible does not teach that such temptations will always painlessly go away through a mysterious process of "trusting God." Unfortunately, the struggle against sexual sin seems to many to be more like sweating bullets than "letting go and letting God." The Bible teaches us that this experience is not surprising. Peter says that we are to "abstain from fleshly lusts which war against the soul" (1 Pet. 2:11). Paul uses the same kind of violent imagery when he says that Christians must "put to death [their] members which are on the earth: fornication, uncleanness, passion, evil desire, and covetousness, which is idolatry" (Col. 3:5).

Now God has provided a very practical help for Christians as they struggle with sexual temptation; that help is called sexual activity. In order to provide satisfactory protection, sexual relations with a spouse should not be infrequent. There needs to be quantitative protection, particularly for the husband. At the same time, the benefit of sexual relations should not be measured merely in terms of frequency or amount. There needs to be qualitative protection, particularly for the benefit of the wife.

If Christian couples come to understand that the ultimate purpose of their marriage is to glorify God, they have taken an important first step. If they then seek to define the secondary purposes of their union as defined in Scripture, they will be equipped to consider the biblical instruction concerning the attitude they should have about marriage, and to receive general and particular instruction from God's Word concerning their duties in the home.

CHAPTER TWO

Headship and Authority

Inescapable Headship

A brief grammar lesson may help explain the nature of biblical authority in the home. When it comes to reading the Scripture, Christians frequently confuse *indicatives* and *imperatives*. An indicative is a statement of fact; there is no *ought* in it—the chair is brown; the ship is tilting; the snow is lumpy. Such statements simply aim to tell us the way things are. An *imperative*, on the other hand, is a command; it tells us what we must do. Close the door! Turn on the computer! Pull over! Consequently, if one were to say, "The book is on the table," this is a simple statement of fact. It is an indicative. But if one said, "Put the book on the table," this is a command—an imperative.

The reason for rehearsing this distinction is that many Christians find themselves misunderstanding what the Bible is saying because *they attempt to turn indicatives into imperatives.* When it comes to the gospel, the carnal heart loves to make this same mistake. What is the gospel but the Great Indicative? Faithful preachers proclaim what God has already done in the cross to save sinners, while sinful men try to turn the gospel message into something they may do to earn salvation.

The same "grammatical" confusion happens when husbands seek to understand the Bible's teaching on headship and authority in marriage. The Bible says the "husband is head of the wife, as also Christ is head of the church"

(Eph. 5:23). Paul most emphatically does *not* say that husbands *ought* to be the heads of their wives. He says that they *are*. In this verse, the apostle is not telling us how marriages ought to function (that comes in the verses following). Rather he is telling us what the marriage relationship between husband and wife *is*. Marriage is *defined* in part as the headship of a husband over a wife. In other words, without this headship, there is no marriage.

This does not mean that God gives no imperatives to the husband. In the verses following we find a very basic imperative indeed—husbands are commanded to love their wives as Christ loved the church. But nowhere is the husband commanded to be a head to his wife. This is because he already is the head of his wife, *by the very nature of marriage*. If he does not love her, he is a poor head, but a head nonetheless.

Meditating on this is a very valuable thing for husbands to do. Because the husband is the head of the wife, he finds himself in a position of *inescapable leadership*. He cannot successfully refuse to lead. If he attempts to abdicate in some way, he may, through his rebellion, lead poorly. But no matter what he does, or where he goes, he does so as the head of his wife. This is how God designed marriage. He has created us as male and female in such a way as to ensure that men will always be dominant in marriage. If the husband is godly, then that dominance will not be harsh; it will be characterized by the same self-sacrificial love demonstrated by our Lord—*Dominus*—at the cross. If a husband tries to run away from his headship, that abdication will dominate the home. If he catches a plane to the other side of the country, and stays there, he will dominate in and by his absence. How many children have grown up in a home *dominated* by the empty chair at the table? If the marriage is one in which the wife "wears the pants," the wimpiness of the husband is the most obvious thing about the marriage, creating a miserable marriage and home. *His abdication dominates*.

In this passage of Ephesians, Paul tells us that husbands, in their role as head, provide a picture of Christ and the church. Every marriage, everywhere in the world, is a picture of Christ and the church. Because of sin and rebellion, many of these pictures are slanderous lies concerning Christ. *But a husband can never stop talking about Christ and church.* If he is obedient to God, he is preaching the truth; if he does not love his wife, he is speaking apostasy and lies—but he is always talking. If he deserts his wife, he is saying that this is the way Christ deserts His bride—a lie. If he is harsh with his wife and strikes her, he is saying that Christ is harsh with the church—another lie. If he sleeps with another woman, he is an adulterer, and a blasphemer as well. How could Christ love someone other than His own Bride? It is astonishing how, for a few moments of pleasure, faithless men can bring themselves to slander the faithfulness of Christ in such a way.

These are difficult words. And even with the qualifications, it is probable that a number of readers have reacted negatively to the earlier use of the word *dominance*. The fact that this is so is simply another testimony to how much the Christian church is influenced by the propaganda of feminism—whether the man-hating secular variety or the sanitized, "evangelical" kind. Nevertheless, the dominance of the husband is a fact; the only choice we have in this regard concerns whether that dominance will be a loving and constructive *dominion* or hateful and destructive *tyranny*. Arguing with the fact of the husband's headship in the home is like jumping off a cliff in order to quarrel with the law of gravity. Marshall the arguments on the way down however one likes, he will eventually find himself refuted in a messy way.

However Christians compromise with feminism, such a compromise cannot undo the *indicative* that God has woven into creation. How could it? God has built the headship of the husband into the very structure of marriage. But what this compromise can do, it does very well—it brings in rebellion and sin. Such rebellion keeps husbands from obeying the *imperative*, which is to love their wives. What is the result? We see husbands denying their status as heads of their wives, and refusing to love them as instructed.

Love and Respect

The second greatest commandment requires that we love our neighbors as ourselves. "And the second, like it, is this: 'You shall love your neighbor as yourself.' There is no other commandment greater than these" (Mark 12:31). And, of course, if we ask "who is our neighbor?" the answer Jesus gives is that the person placed in front of us is our neighbor. As the parable makes clear, this includes the stranger by the side of the road, but it also includes those with whom we live. A husband and wife are certainly required by Scripture to love one another.

But when the Bible gives a specific command to husbands *as husbands*, and does the same for wives *as wives*, the emphasis in the respective commands is notably different. For example, wives are nowhere specifically commanded to love their husbands. In one passage, the older women are urged to teach the younger women to be "husband-lovers." But the word is a compound word (*philandros*), and the form of the word for love refers to a warm affection. The attitude that is required for wives is one of *respect*. ". . . and let the wife see that she respects her husband" (Eph. 5:33).

Men, on the other hand, are commanded to love (*agapao*) their wives to the uttermost. Two examples are given for the men, and both require tremendous self-sacrifice. First, men are to love their wives as they love their own bodies. "So husbands ought to love their own wives as their own bodies; he who loves his wife loves himself" (Eph. 5:28). No one ever hated himself, Paul teaches, and this provides us with a good standard in our treatment of others. A husband should be as solicitous for the welfare of his wife as he is for himself. This is nothing less than the Golden Rule applied to marriage. Second, men are to love their wives as Christ loved the church. "Husbands, love your wives, just as Christ also loved the church and gave Himself for her . . ." (Eph. 5:25).

Now the Scripture plainly gives us our duties. Wives are to respect their husbands, and husbands are to love their wives. But there is more. When we consider these requirements, and look at how men and women relate to one another, we can see the harmony between what God requires, and what we need both to give and to receive.

The commands are given to our respective weaknesses in the performance of our duties. Men need to do their duty with regard to their wives—they need *to love*. Women need to do their duty in the same way—they need *to respect*. But men are generally poor at this kind of loving. C.S. Lewis once commented that women tend to think of love as *taking* trouble for others (which is much closer to the biblical definition), while men tend to think of love as not *giving* trouble to others. Men consequently need work in this area, and they are instructed by Scripture to undertake it. In a similar way, women are fully capable of loving a man, and sacrificing for him, while believing the entire time that he is a true and unvarnished jerk. Women are good at this kind of love, but the central requirement given to wives is that they *respect* their husbands. As Christian women gather together (for prayer? Bible study?), they frequently speak about their husbands in the most *disrespectful* way. They then hurry home to cook, clean, and care for his kids. Why? Because they love their husbands. It is not wrong for the wives to love their husbands, but it is wrong to substitute love for the respect God requires.

We can also see the commands which are given have regard for our respective weaknesses in another way. Men have a need to *be respected*, and women have a need to *be loved*. When Scripture says, for example, that the elders of a church must feed the sheep, it is a legitimate infer-

ence to say that sheep need food. In the same way, when
the Scripture emphasizes that wives must respect their husbands, it is a legitimate inference to say that husbands need
respect. The same is true for wives. If the Bible requires
husbands to love their wives, we may safely say that wives
need to be loved.

But we are often like the man who gave his wife a shot-
gun for Christmas because he wanted one. When a wife is
trying to work on a troubled marriage, she gives to him
what *she* would like, and not what God commanded and
not what he needs. She loves him, and she tells him so. But
does she *respect* him and tell him so?

We have difficulty because we do not follow the scriptural instructions. When a man is communicating his love
for his wife (both verbally and nonverbally), he should be
seeking to communicate to her the security provided by
his covenantal commitment. He will provide for her, he
will nourish and cherish her, he will sacrifice for her, and
so forth. Her need is to be *secure* in his love for her. Her
need is to receive love from him.

When a wife is respecting and honoring her husband,
the transaction is quite different. Instead of concentrating
on the security of the relationship, respect is directed to
his *abilities* and *achievements*—how hard he works, how
faithfully he comes home, how patient he is with the kids,
and so forth.

The specifics may cause problems with some because
he thinks he might *not* come home, and she thinks he doesn't
work nearly hard enough. But love is to be rendered to
wives and respect to husbands, because God has required
it, and not because any husband or wife has earned it. It is
good for us to remember that God requires our spouses
to render to us far more than any of us deserve.

She Was Made for Him

As discussed in the previous chapter, marriage is a creation ordinance; it has been with us since the creation of mankind. When only *half* of humankind had been created, God looked on His work and said, "It is not good that man should be alone; I will make him a helper comparable to him" (Gen. 2:18). When God was creating the world, He stated emphatically at each point that what He had created was good. Everything He did was good until He created man without woman. At that point God said that something was *not* good—it was not good for man to be alone.

The Lord had created Adam and given him a task (Gen. 2:15). In addition to taking care of the Garden of Eden, Adam was also to multiply and replenish the earth. There was an obvious need for a helper as he could not multiply the species all by himself. The task assigned to him was that of exercising dominion over the earth; in order to accomplish this task many descendants were needed. But in addition to the obvious help of making Adam fruitful, Eve was also to accompany him in his vocation and assist him in it.

But the Lord already knew that Adam was going to need this help. The problem did not dawn on God halfway through the creation of man, with the woman then created as an afterthought. The reason the woman was created later was for the purpose of establishing, for all time, the line of authority in the home. Paul applies this lesson very plainly. "For man is not from woman, but woman from man. Nor was man created for the woman, but woman for the man" (1 Cor. 11:8–9).

In other words, the creation order tells us that Adam was not created for Eve, but rather that Eve was created for Adam. Moreover, the way Paul applies this truth shows that the relationship of Adam and Eve was not just unique to them as one couple. As mentioned earlier, they provide a paradigm for all marriages; this pattern is normative for the human race. The point is the intention of God in creation—the case does not rest on *chronological* priority. There are many wives who are older than their husbands (they got here first), but this does not undo the pattern set by the creation of Adam first, and the creation of Eve second.

Paul is making application from the creation order. The application is made to Corinthian men and women, thousands of years after Adam and Eve lived. And although we are living thousands of years after the Corinthians, the fact remains that the order in which Adam and Eve were created was intended for use as a pattern for all subsequent generations of husbands and wives.

This creation order means that all husbands are called to a particular task (in fact, the word *vocation* comes from the Latin verb *voco*, which means *I call*). Their wives are called to the role of aiding and supporting them in their calling. This means, further, that the man is established by God as the authority in the home. Under God, he is defined by the work to which he is called, while she is defined by the man to whom she is called. As they turn to the task, since the work is his responsibility, she is his responsibility as well.

This obviously collides with the idea that men and women both have an equal right to pursue their separate careers as they climb up the professional ladder. Unfortunately, this assumption is common in the evangelical church today. It is thoroughly unbiblical, but this problem was created, not by feminism, but rather by abdicating husbands. One of the central difficulties we face in our culture today is the general "wimping out" of the Christian men. Men have abdicated their God-given strength, leadership, and authority. They do not want to take the masculine role; they do not want to take the initiative because they have taken the easy way out. The fulfillment of the cultural mandate involves hard work, and men need to be hard in order to do the work. This does not mean they are to be hard *on* their wives; it means they are to be hard *for* their wives.

Men and women do not have the same perspective of

work; therefore they do not have the same perspective of authority. This is deeply imbedded in the created order, feminist doctrine notwithstanding. Feminist dogma, engineered by ungodly men, has managed to maneuver multitudes of women into the workforce outside the home. But this has not changed how men and women relate to one another at all. It cannot. Even though the workplace has far more women in it, the authority of men is still firmly intact. With the rhetoric of equality, women have been duped into working outside the home; they have taken a second job and then have been unable to get their husbands to share the load of the first one. She still does the laundry, the cooking, and everything else. And of course the selfish male is the main beneficiary of all this liberation of women; he gets two paychecks for the price of one. He still will take out the garbage, however.

We must confess that God's pattern for the godly authority of a husband over his wife makes sense. The only alternative is ungodly oppression of women by men.

In no way does this mean that women are not competent in many of the tasks they do. A crescent wrench can be used to pound in nails, but that is not what a crescent wrench is *for*. There are some tasks detached from the home in which women do outstanding work. But just because someone is *able* to do a job does not mean that he is called by God to the task. A wife can do many tasks in the home and find fulfillment in doing them. Her husband, confronted with the same job, would be able to do it, but it is like eating gravel for him. He finds no fulfillment; he is not called to the task in the same way she is.

So in 1 Corinthians 11 Paul states a truth which should induce fear and awe in all husbands: *the woman was created to be a helper for the man.* But nothing is more offensive than hearing ignorant men trifle with these truths— making jokes about submission and so forth. Such trifling is completely unbiblical in tone. When a man realizes that he has been created for and called to a particular task, that can be overwhelming in itself (Eph. 2:10). But if he then realizes that he needs *help* in performing that task, and he is not consequently moved with a holy terror, then he is a complete blockhead.

Husbands must, therefore, concentrate on being strong for the sake of their wives. Ungodly men are strong for selfish reasons, and not for the sake of others. A godly husband uses his strength to *give to her*; he does not use his strength to take from her. A properly-ordered relationship is one in which the man knows he was created by God to accomplish a particular task, and he knows that his wife was created by God to help him with that task. He was created for the glory of God, and although it may be frightening to say, she was created *for him* (1 Cor. 11:7, 9).

Responsibility

Given this divinely ordered relationship, we can see that feminism is a very destructive form of false teaching. But we should also be able to see that women are not really the true source of feminism. While it is true that the feminist movement is represented by female spokesmen, they are really nothing more than shills, fronting for a male lie. At the foundation, feminism is the handiwork of two kinds of *men*—destructive, overbearing men on the one hand and wimps on the other. Because of how God made the world, men are always responsible for everything that happens in the feminine world—whether they want that responsibility or not, and whether or not women want to acknowledge it. Consequently, feminism is not the work of dissatisfied women; it is the work of ungodly men.

When a couple comes for marriage counseling, my operating assumption is always that the man is *completely* responsible for *all* the problems. Some may be inclined to react to this, but it is important to note that responsibility is not the same thing as guilt. If a woman has been unfaithful to her husband, of course she bears the guilt of her adultery. But at the same time, he is *responsible* for it.

To illustrate, suppose a young sailor disobeys his orders and runs a ship aground in the middle of the night. The captain and the navigator were both asleep and had nothing to do with his irresponsible actions. Who is finally responsible? The captain and the navigator are responsible for the incident. They are career officers, and their careers are ruined. The young sailor was getting out of the Navy in six months anyway. It may strike many as being unfair, but it is indisputably the way God made the world. The sailor is guilty; the captain is responsible.

Without this understanding of responsibility, authority becomes meaningless and tyrannical. Husbands are responsible for their wives. They are the head of their wives as Christ is the head of the church. Taking a covenant oath to become a husband involves assuming responsibility for that home. This means that *men*, whether through tyranny or abdication, are responsible for any problems in the home.

If Christian men had loved their wives as Christ loved the church, if they had given direction to their wives, if husbands had accepted their wives' necessary help with their God-ordained vocation, there never would have been room for any kind of feminist thinking within the church. Christian men who abdicate their God-given authority, or who feel embarrassed about it, are leaving their wives unprotected.

Weaker Vessels

The Bible gives some very plain instruction to men on how to live with their wives. Oddly enough, the requirement for husbands to be considerate is phrased in a way that makes the modern reader uneasy. "Likewise you husbands, dwell with them with understanding, giving honor to the wife, as to the weaker vessel, and as being heirs together of the grace of life, that your prayers may not be hindered" (1 Pet. 3:7). The Bible says that the wife, in some sense, is the weaker vessel. The husband is, therefore, to *honor* her. He must not abuse her in the subordinate role in which God has placed her. "I will greatly multiply your sorrow and your conception; in pain you shall bring forth children; your desire shall be for your husband, and he shall rule over you" (Gen. 3:16).

Marriage simply amplifies what a person is. Consequently, marriage problems are often created many years before the wedding ceremony. For example, children, while growing up, observe the relationship of their parents to each other. They may also see certain patterns of behavior at school. They hear much teaching, almost all of it false, on the topic of how strength should relate to weakness. And when people receive false teaching, follow poor examples, and then enter into marriage, the results are commonly disastrous.

Peter just assumes as fact that the woman is weaker relative to her husband. Conditioned by feminism, the modern world would dismiss this as a sexist gaffe in a sexist book, and they are at least *partially* correct. Given that "sexism" is a sin, then the Bible is a sinful book. But "sexism" is not a true sin, for sin can only be defined in terms of God's law—it is not determined by the law of man or by the law of woman.

According to the Bible, there is no sin in the fact that men are stronger than women. The sin, if there is sin, lies in whether or not that strength is used according to God's requirements. We must not forget that a few verses earlier, Peter had given husbands this example to follow. "For to this you were called, because Christ also suffered for us, leaving us an example, that you should follow His steps" (1 Pet. 2:21). And a few verses later, he makes this application: "Likewise you wives, be submissive to your own husbands" (1 Pet. 3:1). He then goes on to require the husbands to be likewise considerate. The key word is *likewise*. Husbands and wives are both to be *Christ-like* in their demeanor toward one another. But because of the position in which God has placed him, a man must act differently toward his wife in order to exhibit this attitude than his wife must act toward him.

The problem is that men commonly have trouble honoring "weakness." When men get together with men, some sort of competition usually arises. And when competition is there, men seek to exploit weakness whenever they think they see it. If a football coach were to discover that the other team's left tackle was clearly weak, he will run his plays over the left tackle all night long. So men have this natural tendency, and in our nation, this kind of competitiveness is greatly admired.

Consequently, if there is any kind of problem in the marriage, men commonly fall into an adversarial, competitive relationship with their wives. If they disagree over something, and the distressed wife expresses her concerns, a husband with this basic competitive mentality is going to say, "That is the dumbest thing I ever heard!" He is treating her as though she were the opposing left tackle. When he responds this way, he is seeking to *exploit* her. But Peter does not say to exploit the weakness; he says to *honor* her in it.

So we see a very common disobedience to this passage when men see the weakness of their spouse and then seek to exploit it. A man can be in the midst of the most dreadful sin, which distresses his wife, and he can still bulldoze right over her. She then walks away, feeling as though *she* were the guilty one. Men are tempted to exploit their wives whether they are in the right or not, but especially when they are not. In fact, some men are so much in the grip of their competitiveness that they cannot hear Peter say that women are weaker, in some sense, without thinking that they have somehow "won." But which is better, a five-pound sledge or a china teacup? Which would win a contest between them?

Men respect strength naturally, but they have a hard time respecting weakness. We can see this even on the playground. A couple of boys can get in a fight, one knocks the other down, and the rest of the day they are good friends. The one boy respects the strength of the other, and the other one can respect the fight that the first one put up.

In order for men to respect weakness, they must recognize it as their *own* weakness. A wife with her husband is a joint heir of their mutual inheritance, and her weakness is his weakness. *She is not his adversary.* The weakness is on his *own* team; it is in his *own* family. I was once speaking with a man who seemed greatly pleased at how the children obeyed him, in contrast to their disobedience of his wife. He was pleased that when he said to do something, the children obeyed him, but whenever his wife issued a similar command, they refused. He was acting as though he were in a "discipline foot race" with his wife, and he thought he was winning.

But the fact that the children were not responding to their mother showed there was a deficiency in *his* discipline. Her problem was *his* problem. The husband has a responsibility to make sure that whenever the children even think about talking back to their mother, they see their father's shadow looming behind her. Her weakness must be acknowledged as his, so that his strength may become *her* strength. Her weakness is her strength and may become his strength also. His strength is his weakness, but if overcome, it becomes her strength.

The Level Playing Field

All human cultures are hierarchical. Not everyone has the same amount of talent, brains, beauty, intelligence, or education. The Bible does not require the submission of women to men, but rather of *a* woman to *a* man. The submission of a woman to a man, far from making her submissive to other men, *protects* her from obligations to other men. This provides her with an umbrella of protection (that is, her husband) from other men. She is to be submissive to her *own* husband, and the Bible teaches clearly that no one can serve two masters.

To say a husband should be the leader of his wife is not to say that any and every man is capable of being a spiritual leader, provider, comforter, and protector to any and every woman. Some might argue that the Christian doctrine of submission requires the belief that any man can lead any woman. This is more than false; it is ridiculous.

Women are not created to respond and submit to just anybody. A godly woman is therefore going to limit her range of options. If she understands the Bible, she knows that she was created to be dependent and responsive to *a man*. Now the more God has done for her, and given to her, the more selective she must be. The more a woman excels, the more selective she must be. Some intelligent women have been tempted to play the dunce in order to get a man. This is not right; God has created her to be a help to a *particular* man, and her abilities are something *he* needs—whether or not any other men need them. A godly woman should not lower her standards; marrying a man who does not have the intellectual or spiritual strength to be the leader of the home is just asking for trouble. Abigail did not go well with Nabal.

So the Bible teaches submission of one woman to one man, and not one woman to all men. A woman can cheerfully and graciously acknowledge that a certain man can be a godly Christian leader, but that he is not capable of being that for *her*. The converse of this is that godly men should cheerfully grant that the world contains many women who are, on an individual level, *his betters*. God has created them to be submissive to their *own* husbands.

This hierarchy exists in spite of modern egalitarian dogma. There are God-ordained differences in the world, with values placed on these differences. Is it better to be smart or dumb? Rich or poor? Spiritually rich or spiritually poor? Is it better to be taught in the Scriptures or not taught in the Scriptures? One of our favorite modern expressions reveals our fond wish for a "level playing field." This is a clear indication of envy, and does not at all reflect the way God created the world. Once we make our peace with God-ordained inequities, we can begin to understand how we should proceed.

So a Christian husband should respect the weakness of his wife, treating her as Christ does the church, protecting and watching over her without being condescending. The weakness Peter mentions is God's design, not her fault. *It is not a fault at all.* Weakness is only a fault if it falls short of the design. A china cup is weaker than the five-pound sledge referred to earlier, but a hammer is no good at all for drinking tea.

This does not mean that women have no strength. There are things that godly wives can do which baffle their husbands. Nevertheless, in the marriage relationship, the husband must provide the *foundational* strength. Upon that foundation, the wife is free to develop her strengths in service to her husband. The husband must be a source of strength to his wife even when she knows far more about something than he does. And even when the wife is stronger than the husband in some area, he must be emotionally and spiritually strong enough to assume responsibility in that area.

For example, suppose a husband makes a decision based on information his wife gave him, and the information was in her area of expertise. Suppose further that some disaster occurs as a result. He understands this principle if he takes full responsibility for the resultant problem. But if he abdicates his role as leader, he will say something like, "Why did you. . . ?"

The Servant's Heart

So men and women should marry wisely. A woman should marry a man she respects, and a man should marry a woman he is willing to love and lead with a servant's heart. A man must exercise authority for his wife's sake, and not for his own. He must wield authority with a servant's heart. In John 13:13–17, as Jesus washed the feet of his disciples, He said to them:

> You call Me Teacher and Lord, and you say well, for so I am. If I then, your Lord and Teacher, have washed your feet, you also ought to wash one another's feet. For I have given you an example, that you should do as I have done to you. Most assuredly, I say to you, a servant is not greater than his master; nor is he who is sent greater than he who sent him. If you know these things, happy are you if you do them.

Jesus taught that any Christian who wants to become the greatest must become the servant of all. This certainly applies to the Christian family. The husband must make a conscious decision to utilize his strength for *her* protection and benefit, and not for his own. He can only do that in imitation of Christ. In the Christian family, the way to an understanding of true authority is through *service*.

The Evangelical Husband

"And if it seems evil to you to serve the Lord, choose for yourselves this day whom you will serve, whether the gods which your fathers served that were on the other side of the River, or the gods of the Amorites, in whose land you dwell. But as for me and my house, we will serve the Lord" (Josh. 24:15).

The word *evangelical* used to be descriptive, but in recent years it has been greatly abused. What used to refer to an allegiance to the glorious gospel of Christ is now applied indiscriminately to the modern circus of virtually any subjective religious experience in America. One who uses the word in its older sense must carefully define terms. By *evangelical husband,* I intend to refer to a husband who understands historic Protestant orthodoxy, and who lives in a way that is consistent with that understanding.

The evangelical world is throwing away its theological heritage because of doctrinal faithlessness in Christian homes. It is true that pulpits across our country are filled with a swamp and morass of anecdotes, sentimentalist yawp, yippy-skippy worship, and make-it-up-as-you-go-along theology; but the heads of Christian homes have been willing to have it so. As the expectations for men in the evangelical world have gotten lower, men have not objected—they have breathed a sigh of relief.

But a man who speaks for his house, as Joshua did, must be a man who *teaches* his house, and he must be a man who refuses to submit his family to the foolishness of unbelief—whether the unbelief is dressed up in liberal or pop-evangelical clothes makes little difference. When Jesus teaches us that His sheep will not listen to the voice of a stranger, He is assuming the sheep are right if they do not follow when the voice of the Shepherd is absent (John 10:5).

So the first thing necessary is that a husband must establish his home as a *confessional* home. This means he must know what he believes, and he must communicate and teach this confession of faith to his family. Related to this is the necessity that the confession be *detailed*. A man just saved may be able only to confess that Jesus is Lord—this is enough, many would say. It is certainly enough for salvation (Rom. 10:9–10), but it is *not* enough for a man called to be an instructor for his house. "For though by this time you ought to be teachers, you need someone to teach you again the first principles of the oracles of God; and you have come to need milk and not solid food" (Heb. 5:12). The Bible teaches that a minimalistic approach to doctrine should be an embarrassment for older Christians. The fact that many today glory in having a truncated theology is an occasion of grief. The question is not, "How little can I know and still get to heaven?" The question for husbands is, "Given my time, resources, and abilities, how much can I learn, and how much can I teach my wife and children?"

A man may not be a vocational theologian, but in his

home he must be the *resident* theologian. The apostle Paul, when he is urging women to keep silent in church, tells them that "if they want to learn something, let them ask their own husbands at home" (1 Cor. 14:35). The tragedy is that many modern women have to wonder why the Bible says they should have to ask their husbands. "*He* doesn't know." But a husband must be prepared to answer his wife's doctrinal questions, and if he cannot, then he must be prepared to study so that he can remedy the deficiency. This famous passage is not such a restriction for wives as it is a requirement for husbands. If he doesn't know, he must find out.

Second, he must know *why* he believes as he does so that he can communicate and teach this to his family as well. This is impossible apart from a consistent reading of the Bible, over and over again. In addition to his Bible reading, an evangelical husband must be committed to reading books of solid doctrinal teaching, written by sound, qualified men. Not only must he reflect upon the Word directly, but he should take full advantage of the teachers which God has given to the body of Christ.

As he studies his Bible, he will of course grow in his understanding of the greatness and sovereignty of God in all things. As he does so, he must be humble enough to set aside any erroneous doctrines he has previously held, he must apologize to his family for leading them astray at that point, and he must teach them afresh. Under no circumstances may an evangelical husband cling to error, even if changes are made at a great cost.

In the third place, he must seek to cultivate certain virtues which are built upon this confession of faith. These virtues, or graces, are to be established in the home. The Bible teaches that all doctrine must be lived out, and our manner of living it out must in turn adorn the doctrine.

In a home taught by an evangelical husband, there should be many graces that are simply part of an aroma which is pervasive in the home. Such a man should never speak to his wife without affection and courtesy. He must never lose his temper when correcting the children. When he sins, he should make all appropriate restitution. He must be a rock in his home, a small pebble that somehow by the grace of God pictures the Rock that is Christ.

CHAPTER THREE

Duties of Husbands and Wives

The Privileges of Marital Duty

In thinking about marriage, we tend to think that spontaneous actions are genuine while others performed from a
sense of duty are stifled, artificial, and contrived. We *especially* think this way if we are considering questions "of
the heart." Doing one's duty is thought to be restrictive
to true love.

But the Bible defines love as a whole-hearted keeping
of God's commandments. The greatest act of love was certainly the death of Christ for His people, and that act of
love was not offered on an emotional high. It was a bitter
grief for Christ to drink the cup of God's wrath, but that
grief does not take away from His love for us; rather, it
adds to it.

When we come to our duties gladly, it helps us to discipline our emotions. When we come to our duties with
the knowledge that God has framed them for us and has
assigned all marital duties appropriately, we can rejoice in
His goodness. The result is not a negation of spontaneity,
but rather a disciplining of it.

Biblical Duties of the Husband

In both the Hebrew of the Old Testament, and the Greek
of the New Testament, the word for husband is usually just
the word for "a man," with the context showing that it is a

husband who is in mind. However, another fairly common
word in Hebrew for husband is *baal*, which means "master," or "lord." And in Greek, there are at least two instances
of this sort of usage: *kurios,* which means "lord," and
hupandros, which means "man above." The English word
husband is a wonderful word which encompasses all of these
biblical descriptions of a married man. There is the con-
notation of lordship, but it is a lordship involving great care,
sacrifice, and tenderness.

A husband must always remember that as a husband
he is a living picture of the Lord Jesus. This remembrance
is his first duty in marriage. Since, as a *husband,* a man is
speaking constantly about the Lord's relationship to His
people, he ought to seek to speak *truthfully* as well. The
way the man treats his wife will determine whether he is
speaking the truth about Christ or not. But he does not
have the option of remaining silent; he is speaking all the
time. This is because *the Lord is a husband,* and all husbands are therefore a representation of Him.

Because his relationship is speaking of Christ and the
church all the time, he must learn to imitate Christ in character as well. This points to a man's second duty. The Bible
is very clear that the Lord is a husband to His people: "For
your Maker is your husband, the Lord of hosts is His name"
(Is. 54:5; *cf.* Jer. 31:32; Rev. 21:2; Eph. 5:23). As a man
seeks to imitate the Lord in his duties, he must be a *hus-
bandman* to his wife. This means he must nourish and cherish
her in the same way that he cares for his own body (Eph.
5:29). The word "nourish" is *ektrepho,* which means "to
feed, bring up to maturity." The word "cherish" is *thalpo,*
and means "to keep warm, to cherish with tender love." A
man who does not take particular and tender care of his
wife, and who then expects her to be fruitful and lovely, is
not being a true husband at all; he is a dolt—the Greek word
for this is probably *meathead.* A man must love his wife
sacrificially (Eph. 5:25), and he must not expect anything

but weeds unless he tends the garden with extraordinary care.

This is related to a third duty, which is that of *jealousy*. This perhaps jars our modern sensibilities; we are accustomed to view jealousy as a personal problem, rather than as a virtue to encourage and cultivate. This opinion, or re-action, is simply more evidence of how far we have fallen from biblical convictions concerning marriage. A husband *must* be jealous and protective. Paul uses this image of a good husband to exhort the Corinthian Christians to faithfulness. "For I am jealous for you with godly jealousy. For I have betrothed you to one husband, that I may present you as a chaste virgin to Christ" (2 Cor. 11:2). In following the Lord, Christian men must remember that God's *name* is Jealous. ". . . the Lord, whose name is Jealous, is a jealous God" (Ex. 34:14). It is true that jealousy can be wrong and destructive whenever it is driven by any bitterness, resentment, or malice. But the same could be said for many other attitudes; if mixed with sin, they become sinful! Jealousy does not need to be mixed with sin. And under numerous circumstances, it is a sin *not* to be jealous.

But there are also very mundane duties involved with being a godly husband. For example, a husband must supply his wife with the food she needs. We can see this in a law given to ancient Israel, where a man was not permitted to defraud his first wife of certain marital rights through his polygamy. "If he takes another wife, he shall not diminish her food, her clothing, and her marriage rights. And if he does not do these three for her, then she shall go out free, without paying money" (Ex. 21:10–11). We see here that one of the duties of a husband is to see to it that his wife has the money she needs for *groceries*. Put another way, a man may not shake himself free of certain basic marital obligations simply through taking another woman. It follows that the provision of food *is one of those obligations*. In the New Testament, we see that a man who does not

take care of his extended family is worse than an unbeliever
(1 Tim. 5:8). What then can we say of a man who does not
take care of his immediate family, by neglecting his *wife*?
Neglect of a man's wife in this fashion is the equivalent of
apostasy—it is a denial of Christ, who feeds His bride. In
the same way, the Bible requires that a husband must supply his wife with the *clothing* she needs (Ex. 21:10).

A husband must also meet his wife's sexual needs
(1 Cor. 7:3–4; Ex. 21:10). In this regard, his body belongs
to her. Paul uses very strong language with regard to this;
he says that this is an area where the wife exercises *authority*
over her husband. "Let the husband render to his wife the
affection due her, and likewise also the wife to her husband. The wife does not have authority over her own body,
but the husband does. And likewise the husband does not
have authority over his own body, but the wife does"
(1 Cor. 7:3–4).

As one aspect of this, a husband must not deny his wife
an opportunity to bear children. "And Judah said to Onan,
'Go in to your brother's wife and marry her, and raise up
an heir to your brother.' But Onan knew that the heir would
not be his; and it came to pass, when he went in to his
brother's wife, that he emitted on the ground, lest he should
give an heir to his brother" (Gen. 38:8–9). The Lord struck
Onan down, not because of a particular sexual act, but rather
because of the fraud involved. It is necessary to remember that sexual activity is not seen in the Bible as merely a
recreational indoor sport. It is not just recreation; it is *rec-
reative*. The duty to provide wives with an opportunity for
having children may seem "bizarre" to the modern mind.
But this simply shows us how little modern husbands nourish and cherish their wives.

The Bible is very plain about another duty of husbands
as well. A husband must be *content* with his wife
(Prov. 5:15–23; Matt. 5:28). He is prohibited from cov-
eting the wife of another man. "You shall not covet your
. . . neighbor's wife" (Ex. 20:17). Not only must he not

long after the wife of someone else, he is positively commanded to be content with the wife he has.

> Drink water from your own cistern, and running water from your own well. Should your fountains be dispersed abroad, streams of water in the streets? Let them be only your own, and not for strangers with you. Let your fountain be blessed, and rejoice with the wife of your youth. As a loving deer and a graceful doe, let her breasts satisfy you at all times; and always be enraptured with her love (Prov. 5:15–19).

Specifically, a man is commanded to be satisfied with his wife's breasts and to be enraptured with her love. To compare a woman with others, whether silently or aloud, whether with words or actions, is always destructive. And the more comparisons are made, the less contentment is possible. A husband must be content in *all* areas; consequently, comparisons must be avoided in all areas, whether involving beauty, cooking, intelligence, imagined sexual responsiveness, whatever. For men it is particularly important to be content in the sexual area. This is much easier if a husband is doing what he should be doing in his other areas of responsibility.

Another duty involves the ongoing responsibility that a husband has to review and approve commitments made by his wife.

> Every vow and every binding oath to afflict her soul, her husband may confirm it, or her husband may make it void. Now if her husband makes no response whatever to her from day to day, then he confirms all her vows or all the agreements that bind her; he confirms them, because he made no response to her on the day that he heard them. But if he does make them void after he has heard them, then he shall bear her guilt (Num. 30:13–15).

We should recognize that when a husband says nothing, he is approving and leading *by default*. Whether he speaks or is silent, a man cannot cease being the head of the home. He can do it badly or well, but he cannot escape from the responsibility God has placed upon him.

Biblical Duties of Wives

In any discussion of a wife's duties, we must understand the context of these duties. The previous section did not just give us "the husbands' part," with this section giving us "the wives' part." Rather, all the responsibilities for wives listed below can legitimately be added to the husbands' list of responsibilities. Not only is he responsible before God to do *his* job, he is responsible before God to see that she does hers. And of course, this is not done by bossing her around. It is done through nourishing and cherishing her.

First, as noted previously, a wife must respect her husband (Eph. 5:22, 33). The fundamental duty of the husband is to love his wife. By way of contrast, the fundamental duty of the wife is to *respect* her husband. Man and woman are oriented to one another so differently that their fundamental duties to one another are different as well. Respect in this situation entails both *honor* and *obedience*. Now of course wives are to love their husbands because the Bible requires all believers to love their neighbors as themselves. But when the Bible turns to particular *wifely* duties, the *emphasis* is upon respect and not love.

A wife should also, under the providence of God, bear children. "Nevertheless she will be saved in childbearing if they continue in faith, love, and holiness, with self-control" (1 Tim. 2:15). Furthermore, she should nurture those children, and care for them with great tenderness. "But we were gentle among you, just as a nursing mother cherishes her own children" (1 Thess. 2:7). This is not just given as an example; it is positively commanded—"admonish the young women to love their husbands, to love their children" (Titus 2:4).

A wife must not *complain* in her fruitfulness. The fruitfulness of childbearing and childrearing is frequently very hard work. How could it *not* be? Nevertheless, it is God's doing (Gen. 3:16), and it is the wife's duty to submit to the will of God and gladly bear children for her husband.

Incidentally, she should not *boast* in her fruitfulness either. All boasting should be in the Lord. Sometimes, in reaction to the "anti-children" mentality of the modern world, some Christian women have taken to bearing children almost as an act of defiance and rebellion. But we must not be reactionaries against the world; rather, we must all live before the Lord. The biblical response to fruitfulness is that of *gladness*.

The Bible also gives wives the duty of being industrious in the home. Paul instructs Titus to have "the older women [be] teachers of good things—that they admonish the young women to love their husbands, to love their children, to be discreet, chaste, homemakers, good, obedient to their own husbands, that the word of God may not be blasphemed" (Titus 2:3–5). The instruction is that the younger women are to be homemakers, involved in domestic pursuits. Not only are they to *be* home, they are to be *productive* at home. Industry in the home means hard work in cleaning, cooking, child-rearing, and so forth. *It is possible to disobey God through neglect of the dishes.*

Of course this is hard work, especially when the little ones are young. Many wives, when they go through this experience, are tempted to treat "being tired" as though it were a symptom of having done something wrong. Rather, it is a symptom of having done many things *right*.

If a woman is competent, and she should be, *in due time* her industry will take her outside the home (Prov. 31:10–31). The Bible does not teach that the woman's place is in the home; it requires that the home be her *priority*, but she is not at all limited to the home.

A related duty requires that a wife keep the home well-supplied with food and clothing. "She is like the merchant ships, she brings her food from afar. . . . She is not afraid of snow for her household, for all her household is clothed with scarlet" (Prov. 31:14, 21). If her husband works hard to supply her with money for these needs, as he is required to do, then she must be a responsible *steward* of what he gives. She is not to be frivolous. Shopping should be treated, not as entertainment and luxury, but as work. As a steward involved in work, she must be diligent.

A wife must meet her husband's sexual needs (1 Cor. 7:2–5). This involves more than just being "willing" whenever "he wants it;" it involves being a *responsive* lover.

> Like an apple tree among the trees of the woods, so is my beloved among the sons. I sat down in his shade with great delight, and his fruit was sweet to my taste. He brought me to the banqueting house, and his banner over me was love. Sustain me with cakes of raisins, refresh me with apples, for I am lovesick. His left hand is under my head, and his right hand embraces me. I charge you, O daughters of Jerusalem, by the gazelles or by the does of the field, do not stir up nor awaken love until it pleases (Song 2:3–7).

God has given the sexual relationship in marriage as a protection against immorality. It is important that this purpose be remembered, especially by wives. Women have a tendency to be insulted at their husbands' temptations, and an insulted and offended wife is no protection at all.

A wife must carefully avoid nagging and arguing. We are told the "contentions of a wife are a continual dripping" (Prov. 19:13). Solomon also reminds us that a "continual dripping on a very rainy day and a contentious woman are alike; whoever restrains her restrains the wind, and grasps oil with his right hand" (Prov. 27:15–16). God has given women great abilities with the tongue, and they must use this ability to *help* their husbands. A wise woman knows the power of her words, and so conforms them to the Word of God. "She opens her mouth with wisdom, and on her tongue is the law of kindness (Prov. 31:26). A foolish woman just thinks the house needs the constant background noise, and tears the place down with her tongue.

The Bible also teaches that a wife should be a *disciple* of her husband. "Let your women keep silent in the churches, for they are not permitted to speak; but they are to be submissive, as the law also says. And if they want to learn something, let them ask their own husbands at home; for it is shameful for women to speak in church" (1 Cor. 14:34–35). A husband should be instructing and teaching his wife. She should not make this duty of his superfluous by going elsewhere for the instruction. There is no inconsistency between submission and intelligence. In this regard it is good for wives to remember Abigail, a beautiful, submissive, and *intelligent* woman (1 Sam. 25:3,41).

A Christian wife should be hard-working in works of charity. On this the Bible is really quite plain. When Paul is considering the kind of widow who may be supported by the Christian church, he sets the standard high.

> Do not let a widow under sixty years old be taken into the number, and not unless she has been the wife of one man, well reported for good works: if she has brought up children, if she has lodged strangers, if she has washed the saints' feet, if she has relieved the afflicted, if she has diligently followed every good work (1 Tim. 5:9–10).

We also have the example of the productivity of the ideal wife of Proverbs. "She extends her hand to the poor, yes, she reaches out her hands to the needy" (Prov. 31:20).

A woman who understands all these duties, and labors faithfully at them, is frankly a woman who is *priceless.* Her husband has received a great blessing, as he well knows. So have the children, and all who come into contact with that household. "Who can find a virtuous wife? For her worth is far above rubies" (Prov. 31:10).

CHAPTER FOUR

Efficacious Love

Love Bestows Loveliness

A common assumption in the world is that women must "keep themselves up" in order to keep a man. In the world of attracting and being attracted, women are taught to view themselves as being primarily responsible for their own attractiveness, or loveliness. This viewpoint is inculcated early. Once young girls used to play with baby dolls, seeing themselves in the role of the nurturing mother; now they can be seen playing with Barbie dolls, seeing themselves *in the place of the doll*. And of course, the doll is both pretty, and stacked. The pressure is on and stays on.

The perversion in this is not that women desire to be attractive or lovely. The perversion is the modern divorce of a woman's loveliness from the behavior of her father and husband. There is nothing wrong with wanting a lovely garden; there is a great deal of folly in wanting a lovely garden which will tend and keep itself. The Bible teaches that a Christian husband is responsible for the loveliness of his wife. Before she is married, her father is responsible for that loveliness. When she marries, her husband assumes this responsibility. The husband's example in this loving is Jesus Christ.

> Husbands, love your wives, just as Christ also loved the church and gave Himself for her, that He might sanctify and cleanse her with the washing of water by the

> word, that He might present her to Himself a glorious
> church, not having spot or wrinkle or any such thing,
> but that she should be holy and without blemish
> (Eph. 5:25–27).

God therefore requires husbands to love their wives *with
effect*. In loving our wives, we are not to imitate the *senti-
mental* loving of that modern idol, "gentle jesus," but rather
we are to imitate the *efficacious* loving of the Lord Jesus
Christ who came to earth in order to purchase His people,
and save them from their sins. In the grace of God, Christ
made His people lovely; He did not find them lovely—"For
when we were still without strength, in due time Christ
died for the ungodly. For scarcely for a righteous man will
one die; yet perhaps for a good man someone would even
dare to die. But God demonstrates His own love toward
us, in that while we were still sinners, Christ died for us"
(Rom. 5:6–8). Christ came, and suffered, in order to *secure* the salvation of His people from their sins. He did
not come in order to *try* to save them.

So when a man takes a woman into his home, all who
know them should expect to see her flourish and grow in
loveliness in the years to come. If their wedding ceremony
referred at all to the fifth chapter of Ephesians, was this
not what he vowed he would do? As a husband treats his
wife in the scriptural fashion, he should expect her to grow
increasingly lovely. This is not because the husband has
earned it, but rather because through the grace of God, he
has been blessed. The only one who produces any kind of
growth is God Himself (1 Cor. 3:6). But the sovereign God
uses His appointed means, and His appointed means for
the cultivation of loveliness in wives is thoughtful, self-
sacrificial love on the part of husbands.

In this passage of Ephesians, Paul does not require that
husbands imitate the Lord in His *sentiment* toward His
church; they are to imitate Him in His actions toward her.
And those actions are efficacious. They accomplish something. In this imitation, the husband is required, first, to

"give himself for her." He is to imitate how Christ sanctifies and cleanses the church, and he is to apply in his small way, the washing of water by the word. He should do so seeking to present her to himself as a glorious and beautiful woman. No husband is sufficient for these things, and yet the grace of God is strong and powerful, and can work in sinful husbands, and can transform sinful marriages. An acknowledgment of God's required pattern of imitation for marriage is the necessary starting point. It is crucial that husbands come to see that they must assume full responsibility for the loveliness of their wives.

The Fact of Physical Beauty

I will discuss the importance of *inward* beauty in the next section. But because we live in a culture that is obsessed with external beauty, Christians have sometimes reacted and thought that any consideration of physical beauty is "worldly," and that Christians should be concerned solely with spiritual qualities. And because we live in a time when egalitarianism is rampant, other Christians have objected that to look for certain ideals of feminine beauty is "unfair." Both approaches can seem very spiritual and very holy. But in fact, this is not spiritual Christianity at all. On the one hand, it is a gnostic disparagement of the material world; and on the other, it is an envious rebellion against the way God made the world.

A brief consideration of many scriptural passages demonstrates that there is such a thing as feminine beauty. Abraham, for example, had a beautiful wife. "And it came to pass, when he was close to entering Egypt, that he said to Sarai his wife, 'Indeed I know that you are a woman of *beautiful* countenance'" (Gen. 12:11). When they got into Egypt, the response of the Egyptians showed that Abraham was not making things up. "So it was, when Abram came into Egypt, that the Egyptians saw the woman, that she was *very beautiful*" (Gen. 12:14).

Isaac also married a beautiful woman: "Now the young woman was *very beautiful to behold*, a virgin . . ." (Gen. 24:16). She was in fact so beautiful that Isaac resorted to a similar deception as used by Abraham concerning his wife's relationship to himself—for the sake of safety (Gen. 26:7).

When it came to this general subject, the patriarchs knew what they were doing; Jacob also loved a beautiful woman. He was tricked into marrying Leah, but his first choice was Rachel. "Leah's eyes were delicate, but *Rachel was beautiful of form and appearance*" (Gen. 29:17). This biblical record of the stunning beauty of the wives of Abraham, Isaac, and Jacob is important to remember when we later come to Peter's teaching on the subject of beauty, and the holy women of the "former times." The beauty that came from the gentle and quiet spirit was not the biblical equivalent of having a "nice personality." It was connected to an external beauty—one that captivated husbands, and, at times, stumbled others.

God also refers to feminine beauty in some of Israel's captives. He speaks this way: ". . . and you see among the captives *a beautiful woman*, and desire her and would take her for your wife . . ." (Deut. 21:11).

The historical record of Scripture also gives us an account of a first-class mismatch mentioned previously. Nabal was a blockhead, who had a wife who was frankly out of his league. Abigail was both beautiful and intelligent. "The name of the man was Nabal, and the name of his wife Abigail. And she was a woman of good understanding *and beautiful appearance*; but the man was harsh and evil in his doings" (1 Sam. 25:3).

David was lured into adultery and a murderous cover-up because Bathsheba was beautiful. "Then it happened one evening that David arose from his bed and walked on the roof of the king's house. And from the roof he saw a woman bathing, and the woman was *very beautiful to behold*" (2 Sam. 11:2).

There are other scriptural examples as well. Absalom's

daughter, Tamar, was of beautiful appearance (2 Sam. 14:27). Scripture agrees with the assessment of the great Persian king; Queen Vashti was a beautiful woman (Esther 1:11). The woman who replaced her, Hadassah or Esther, was also lovely and beautiful (Esther 2:7). Job's daughters were not only beautiful, they were more beautiful than all the women in the land (Job 42:15). The bride of Song of Solomon is also "beautiful as Tirzah, lovely as Jerusalem, awesome as an army with banners" (Song 6:4). God compares the unfaithful nation of Israel to a very beautiful woman, seduced and led away by her own beauty (Ezek. 16).

This may all seem like a belaboring of the obvious— "everyone knows there are pretty women"—but it is an important point for husbands to understand. When husbands undertake the assigned responsibility of loving their wives in such a way that they grow in loveliness, they need to understand that the results will be *visible*. This does not mean that, with the right husband, all woman could be equally beautiful. Some women have the advantage of a greater natural beauty, and others had exceptional fathers—men who treated their daughters right. But it does mean that a man who marries biblically should expect his wife to be visibly lovelier on their tenth anniversary—and if she is not, he knows that *he* is the one responsible. But as the one responsible, he has to know where true beauty begins.

True Beauty

Jesus compared the Pharisees to *beautiful* tombs that were full of corruption on the inside. "Woe to you, scribes and Pharisees, hypocrites! For you are like whitewashed tombs which indeed appear beautiful outwardly, but inside are full of dead men's bones and all uncleanness" (Matt. 23:27). From beginning to end, the Bible teaches us that man looks on the outward appearance, and that God sees the heart. But in Scripture, the heart is not set forth as the only point worth considering, but rather as the starting point. True feminine beauty does not begin and end with the heart; rather, it begins with the heart and it ends with a true external adornment.

So while we must not accept the pagan notion that only the "spiritual" has any value, we must guard ourselves against the opposite pagan snare as well. This is the idea that *only* the material and external has any value, and that the internal spiritual beauty is irrelevant. The assumption is that if only a woman gets the right skin moisturizer, uses the right makeup, dresses well, keeps herself trim, and so on, *ad infinitum*, then she will be beautiful. The Bible teaches that it is not necessarily so—a beautiful woman without discretion presents the same kind of incongruity as lipstick on a camel (Prov.11:22). The Bible also flatly prohibits Christian women from taking this externalized approach to beauty.

Paul, for example, teaches that Christian "women adorn themselves in modest apparel, with propriety and moderation, not with braided hair or gold or pearls or costly clothing" (1 Tim. 2:9). It is important to notice that he is not prohibiting adornment; rather, he is requiring women to adorn themselves in a certain kind of way. He is prohibiting a certain kind of ostentatious display. In the first century, women would braid jewels into their hair, or sprinkle gold dust on it. This kind of "strutting one's stuff" was obnoxious to Paul, it is obnoxious today, and was equally offensive to the prophet Isaiah. He apparently saw some of the daughters of Zion, thoroughly spoiled, and cruising the mall. "Moreover the Lord says: 'Because the daughters of Zion are haughty, and walk with outstretched necks and wanton eyes, walking and mincing as they go, making a jingling with their feet . . .'" (Is. 3:16). Because they were proud and arrogant in their external beauty, the Lord vowed to take away their hair (v. 17), their dignity (v. 17), their finery (v. 18), ankle bracelets (v. 18), scarves and crescents (v. 18), pendants, bracelets, and veils (v. 19), headdresses (v. 20), leg ornaments and headbands (v. 20), perfume boxes and charms (v. 20), rings (v. 21), nose jewelry (v. 21), clothing for festivals (v. 22), cloaks and outer garments (v. 22), purses (v. 22), mirrors (v. 23), fine linen (v. 23), turbans and robes (v. 23).

In other words, when women are beautiful and unholy, their beauty is a provocation to the Lord. "And so it shall be: Instead of a sweet smell there will be a stench; instead of a sash, a rope; instead of well-set hair, baldness; instead of a rich robe, a girding of sackcloth; and branding instead of beauty" (Is. 3:24). God is not mocked; He hates beauty when it is internally ugly. Moreover, He will bring the outside to match the internal pollution.

Conversely, when a woman is lovely in her spirit, that loveliness cannot be contained. It enchants her husband—even some husbands who do not fear God.

> Wives, likewise, be submissive to your own husbands, that even if some do not obey the word, they, without a word, may be won by the conduct of their wives, when they observe your chaste conduct accompanied by fear. Do not let your adornment be *merely outward*—arranging the hair, wearing gold, or putting on fine apparel—rather let it be the hidden person of the heart, with the *incorruptible beauty* of a gentle and quiet spirit, which is very precious in the sight of God. For in this manner, in former times, the holy women who trusted in God also *adorned themselves*, being submissive to their own husbands, as Sarah obeyed Abraham, calling him lord, whose daughters you are if you do good and are not afraid with any terror (1 Pet. 3:1–6).

Now this internal gentleness is something Peter urges upon the wives. But taking the teaching of all of Scripture into account, we can see that a woman concentrates on this under the loving oversight of her husband. As he loves her, she bears fruit. As she bears this fruit, it delights him. In this delight he loves her more, and she bears more fruit. The wife is to cooperate fully, receiving his love, but he is the one responsible to give it.

Courtesy

A biblical husband must seek to cultivate the loveliness of
his wife in all things, whether they seem great or small. One
area which seems small to modern men is the practice of
courtesy to women. In the book of Romans, the apostle Paul
instructed all Christians on the obligation we have to be
courteous to one another. "Let love be without hypocrisy.
Abhor what is evil. Cling to what is good. Be kindly affec-
tionate to one another with brotherly love, *in honor giving preference to one another . . .*" (Rom. 12:9).

Peter requires that husbands behave with a thoughtful
and courteous consideration of their wives. "Likewise you
husbands, dwell with them with understanding, *giving honor*
to the wife, as to the weaker vessel, and as being heirs together of the grace of life, that your prayers may not be
hindered" (1 Pet. 3:7).

But modern American husbands have fallen into a trap
of leveling and reductionism. This reductionism shows itself in an egalitarian tendency in the area of manners or
courtesy. Everyone must be the same, and everything must
be identical. We do not think we are required to defer (with
some visible indication of deference) in any way to anyone else. Consequently, there are many people today who
have never shown an act of honor and deference to *anyone*. In such a cultural climate, it is not surprising that there
are many husbands who have never honored their wives.

If a Christian man is asked about it, he may say he does
honor and respect his wife in his heart. But the Bible doesn't
require us to honor and respect people in our *hearts*. It requires us to honor and respect them. The heart is obviously where it all must begin, but if it never shows up in
external behavior, it is not a biblical honor and respect. Biblical honor must show up in verbal and visible demonstra-
tions that proceed from the heart, but are not locked up
in the heart.

Because we are creatures, and because God has divided
us into various nations and cultures, the marks of respect

and honor we show will vary from culture to culture. Obviously, there is not a biblical problem with these cultural differences. But the requirement to honor is not so easily dispensed with. For example, in the British military they salute differently than in our military. The Bible does not tell us which form of saluting must be used, but it *does* require such a thing as a salute. Scripture requires us to demonstrate our deference. There is no such thing as *invisible* honor or respect.

We are all sinners and under the wrath of God by nature. But if God has changed us, that new creation is going to be visibly manifest in the world, just as the old man was visibly manifest. A husband cannot say, "All my behavior notwithstanding, I still honor my wife, even though I never show it." Husbands must honor their wives.

This is a demonstration within marriage of an attitude which we should see elsewhere in the church.

> And those members of the body which we think to be less honorable, on these we bestow greater honor; and our unpresentable parts have greater modesty, but our presentable parts have no need. But God composed the body, having given greater honor to that part which lacks it, that there should be no schism in the body, but that the members should have the same care for one another (1 Cor. 12:23–25).

The Bible requires that the strong honor and respect the weak. But in the world, the strong take advantage of the weak. In the church, the strong are to respect the weak. This does not change the basic line of authority that God has created. Heads of households must be respected by their wives; there is a biblical obligation for wives to submit to their husbands. Scripture does not reverse our definitions of strength and weakness. But the thing that is unique about Christianity is that the honor and respect are required in *both* directions. It is natural for the weak to honor the strong. But for the strong to honor the weak requires grace from God.

Over the years, our culture has built up a number of ways to display this kind of honor. Many of these expressions of honor have been almost completely destroyed over the last several decades. Displays of cultural honor and respect have disintegrated in most of the contemporary world. With regard to marriage, it is a scriptural responsibility of Christian husbands to recover it. The recovery may be awkward and difficult, but it is better than making up some display of honor and respect *ex nihilo*. And although they have taken a beating, there are still some things that are deeply rooted in our culture, and which *can* be successfully recovered. Christian husbands need to begin the recovery of courteous habits in their treatment of their wives.

Here we get into the area of etiquette or love in trifles, love in the little things. The reductionists will say, "It doesn't make any difference if a husband always opens the car door for his wife." Certainly, in the cosmic scheme of things, God does not command husbands to open their wives' car doors. But He does command husbands to honor their wives. And how does the husband obey this command and display to her and to the world that he honors and respects her, if not by what he says and *does*? No one particular cultural pattern of behavior is biblically required.

This means men must honor their wives in tangible ways. "What! Do you mean I have to walk all the way around the car?" Yes—and car doors are just a small part of it. He must honor her in front of their children, and insist that they imitate him in that honor. By his words and actions, he should constantly praise and honor her in public (Prov. 31:28).

We cannot begin this revolution in manners by demanding that the people who owe *us* respect start showing it. It will begin when we start to show respect and honor where we need to show it. When this kind of honor is cultivated, the results are beautiful. They are part of a husband's cultivation of his wife's loveliness and beauty, for which he is responsible. Much has been lost; we are going to have trouble getting back to such cultural standards without some awkwardness. Nevertheless, we must remember that the heart of true courtesy is in how we treat other people. And the best place a man can begin to recover such consistent charity is in how he treats his wife.

Romantic Love

In his book *The Allegory of Love*, C.S. Lewis commented on the tradition of romantic love in Western culture. He said:

> If the thing at first escapes our notice, this is because we are so familiar with the erotic tradition of modern Europe that we mistake it for something natural and universal and therefore do not inquire into its origins. . . . It seems . . . a natural thing that love (under certain conditions) should be regarded as a noble and ennobling passion: it is only if we imagine ourselves trying to explain this doctrine to Aristotle, Virgil, St. Paul, or the author of *Beowulf*, that we become aware how far from natural it is.

The previous section addressed the importance of courteous love within Christian marriage. This was done first because the Bible teaches it (and it *is* important), but also as a preparation for the minefield we will walk through now. This is the minefield of the Bible's teaching on romantic love.

Romantic love, as it is commonly understood, is a modern idol of the mind, emotions, and heart. Because many husbands and wives serve this idol, it is not surprising that it causes great dissatisfaction within marriages, hopeless expectations, quarrels, fights, and, of course, divorces. Idolatry occurs whenever we look to a created thing with the expectation that it be and do what only the living God can be and do. This particular idolatry is that of confusing a very normal (but transient) emotional/biological reaction with the abiding and obedient love that Christ gives.

Courtesy, honor, and visible love are certainly required of husbands in Scripture. Warmth and tenderness toward wives are also required. But even in saying this, our modern misunderstanding of love is illustrated. A very common reaction to this way of phrasing things could be, "*Required*? Warmth and tenderness are *required*? But shouldn't such things be spontaneous and natural?" No.

When husbands obey God in how they treat their wives, their homes are pleasant places to be, and their wives are nourished. But this consistent practice of *caritas*—costly love—in the home is not the same thing as the initial glow that we call "falling in love." It is another thing entirely.

We are told, and not just by a few, that Christians must be able to keep that "romantic spark" within their marriages. If this means simply that Christians should have good marriages, the point is fine, and we shouldn't quibble about words. But it often is intended to mean that Christians should expect and demand the same level and intensity of that initial romantic thrill to last throughout a marriage, and that if it does not, something is seriously wrong.

Two basic problems show the weakness of this understanding. The first is the emotional impossibility of retaining "very first time" sensations throughout the course of a relationship. Relationships are supposed to mature. This maturing means growth and improvement, not the constant buzz of the initial rush.

The second problem is that it overlooks the differing assumptions about the nature of relationships which God has built into His sons and daughters. The Bible teaches that men and women are oriented to one another differently. "For man is not from woman, but woman from man. Nor was man created for the woman, but woman for the man" (1 Cor. 11:8–9). The prepositions in these verses are important. The woman was created *for* the man. The man was not created *for* the woman. Now Paul is telling us

here about how God made us. His instruction elsewhere
about what we are to do as men and women is based on
what we are as men and women, and how we are oriented.
The fundamental orientation of an obedient man is to his
calling or vocation under God. Under normal circumstances,
he cannot fulfill his calling alone—he needs help. The fundamental orientation of an obedient woman is to give that
help. Another way of saying this is that the man's orientation is to do the job with her help, while the woman's orientation is to help him do the job. He is oriented to the
task, and she is oriented to him.

Now what does this have to do with romance? When a
man first undertakes to court a woman, it *appears* that he
is oriented the same way she is. Courting and marrying are
simply his current task, but she may assume his behavior
reflects a shared permanent orientation. And a short time
after they marry, she is left wondering what happened to
him and all that romantic attention he was willing to give
her. But he, having finished the "task" of getting a wife, is
now foolishly neglecting her and has moved on to other
tasks.

She is discontent because she thinks that her orientation should govern the relationship. He is oblivious to her
discontent because he thinks his orientation should govern the relationship. They are both wrong. She wants him
to spend far more time devoted directly to her. He wants
to spend more time than he ought to on the job. She has
the traditional (and saccharine) assumption that a man and
woman are made by God to have the same orientation toward one another—that of gazing into one another's eyes
until the screen fades to black. He, on the other hand, wants
to spend far less time loving her than the Bible requires.

In other eras, the masculine expectations of the marriage relationship were normative. In our day, the feminine
expectation is the normative one. This does not mean that
women get what they expect, but simply that feminine expectations govern what our culture as a whole calls "a good

marriage." But both these approaches are wrong. As Christians, we must conform to the biblical standards and norms. It should not surprise us that the Bible forbids the tyranny of masculine expectations, as well as the usurpation of feminine expectations—and places each set of expectations in their proper place.

Obviously, this truth must not be used by any Christian husband as an excuse for neglecting his wife and family. Her orientation toward him is God-given; it is this which makes her so capable of helping him in the task which God has called him to do. If he neglects her, he is really destroying himself. He who loves his wife loves himself (Eph. 5:28). But it is equally important for the man to not neglect his vocation—what he has been called to do under God.

So a husband and wife are not to be shoulder-to-shoulder, marching off to work at the task together. Nor are they both to be at home all the time, face-to-face, eternally and perpetually "in love." Rather, with both man and woman understanding their respective roles, he faces his future and calling under God, and she, by his side, faces him.

Men are to love their wives as Christ loved His wife—self-sacrificially. They are to do so knowing that love, scripturally understood, is not a sentiment or emotion, but rather a series of actions which transform. Biblical love is efficacious. They are to love their wives, knowing that this is going to have an effect in the realm of the spirit. As a wife cultivates a gentle and quiet spirit, she becomes increasingly beautiful. He treats her in the way of Christ in all things, both great and little. She grows in beauty, and this beauty is alluring to her husband. But it is not the same thing as the infatuation they both felt when they first got together—it cannot be. It is far more mature than this. It must therefore not be confused with romantic love; it is far, far better.

CHAPTER FIVE

Keeping Short Accounts

The Problem of Sin

Our problem is that husbands and wives are sinners. Marriage problems are overwhelmingly problems with *sin*— lack of conformity to the Word of God in our thoughts, words, and actions. And when we are not in step with the Word, those closest to us, those who are members of our families, notice the problems first.

This means that a marriage is in trouble if the couple does not know how to deal both with temptation and sin. In order for a marriage to be healthy, both husband and wife must understand what sin is, what God's provision for sin in the cross was, and what to do when they sin against God in the marriage relationship. An important part of the modern departure from the biblical understanding of marriage is a glossing over the problem of sin. Consequently, an important part of the reformation of marriage must be a return to biblical confession of sin.

Keeping short accounts means that an individual does not postpone confession of sin if confession is necessary. This applies in the first place to a person's relationship to God. If someone is not confessing sin to God, he will not be able to apologize properly to others. Sin should be confessed as soon as it is understood to be sin. "If we confess our sins, He is faithful and just to forgive us our sins and to cleanse us from all unrighteousness" (1 John 1:9).

When sins are confessed, it is like picking something

up that was dropped on the carpet. If a person learns to pick things up immediately, a thousand things can be dropped on the carpet, and the home will still remain clean. But if things are only picked up once every six months, the result will be an overwhelming house cleaning job. To continue the illustration, some homes are so messed up that those responsible for cleaning simply do not know where to start. They do not necessarily like the way it is, but they are simply overwhelmed. But such things always accumulate *one at a time*. If they had been picked up as fast as they had been dropped, then the home would have remained clean.

In the same way, "things" need to be picked up in all relationships. Confession of wrongdoing should always occur *immediately*. "He who covers his sins will not prosper, But whoever confesses and forsakes them will have mercy" (Prov. 28:13). Nothing good was ever accomplished through postponement of confession. If something is dropped on the floor now, it should be picked up now. Short accounts must be kept; in relationships it is necessary to avoid putting off confession.

In this teaching of confession it is important to emphasize that at conversion, our sins are forgiven, and we are completely justified. Our justification, our standing as forgiven men and women, is never altered by anything we do or do not do, including whether or not we confess our sins. A true child of God is perfect in Christ regardless of his behavior. But refusal to confess sin does affect the quality of a person's *enjoyment* of his justification. When David fell into his grievous sin of adultery and murder, he was a justified man the entire time. But he certainly was not walking in the joy of his salvation. "Restore to me the *joy* of Your salvation . . ." (Ps. 51:12). The fact of his relationship to God was not threatened, but his experience in that relationship was one of misery until he confessed his sin.

In the same way, many Christians drift into unconfessed sin, and lose the joy of their salvation. As they continue in sin, they become more and more miserable in this joyless condition. During this same time, they are also going to church, learning the songs and hymns, along with all the jargon, smiling and shaking hands hypocritically, pretending to be in the joy of the Lord. It never occurs to them that half these people are pretending in the same way as they are. And, of course, periodically a brand new Christian comes bubbling into the church, and discovers all the older "more mature" Christians slumped over in the pews muttering, "Just wait, *he'll* learn." There is something fundamentally wrong with this. Unconfessed sin robs Christians of their joy in a delightful relationship with their Father in heaven. This is seen very clearly in our relationship to God.

But the same principle applies to all other relationships as well, including the relationships within the family. If a child is out of fellowship with his parents, that child does not cease to be the parents' child. The *fact* of the relationship is untouched. But sin certainly does affect the quality of the relationship—it takes away the joy of that relation. If unacknowledged sin is allowed to accumulate, it interferes with relationships more and more.

In the marriage relationship, the same principle applies. Suppose a man comes home from work and his wife cheerfully greets him. He had a bad day, so he snaps at her and stomps off into the living room. He reads the paper, glowering for ten minutes. At that point, he cannot calm down, walk into the kitchen and say, "Hi, hon, what's for dinner?" He cannot act as though nothing happened. His sin affects the joy of the relationship. The *fact* of their relationship is not affected—they are still husband and wife—but the quality of it *is* affected. There can be no genuine fellowship between them until that sin is addressed. But how should sin be addressed?

Putting Things Right

Once we realize that confession is necessary, we still must learn *how* to confess and apologize. Tragically, many who need to apologize to their spouse for numerous offenses do not do anything more than hint around the edges. But true apologies are good for us; they build us up in the Christian faith.

One of the best ways to discipline oneself when it comes to prevention of sin is to make thorough restitution. First, restitution is necessary in its own right. If an item is stolen, not only should the act be confessed to God, the item must then be returned to its rightful owner. Confession of sin does not transfer property rights; it does not make the stolen goods the possession of the thief. Second, the humbling that results from making restitution is equally good for the soul. Restitution is so humbling that it really teaches us to think twice before sinning in that way again.

So if a man yells at his wife, reading the paper and calming down a little bit *does not repair the situation*. When Zacchaeus was converted, he vowed to make restitution. Within marriage, a most important form of restitution is that of a godly apology. But married couples can easily fall into a pattern of apologizing which is geared more to saving face than it is geared to putting things right with the other person.

Furthermore, the other person often goes along with the charade because he does not know how to extend true forgiveness any more than the one who sinned knows how to apologize. Forgiveness presupposes genuine wrongdoing on the part of the other person. The difficulty is that we have a hard time forgiving genuine wrongdoing. This is why people apologize as though the "real me" was not the culprit. "I'm sorry. I was angry and said some things I didn't mean." This is relatively easy to forgive *because the other person didn't mean it*. But sin can only be forgiven when the person *did* mean it—it is then *sin*, and can be forgiven. The one apologizing should have said, "I was wrong in what I said and did this morning. I was angry, and I shouldn't have been. I said those things because I wanted to hurt you. At the time, I meant what I said, and what I said and meant was offensive to God and hurtful to you. Would you please accept my apology?" This is a real apology, and it paves the way for a real restoration of fellowship in the relationship. It is also humbling and hard to do.

If the husband and wife have been at odds for a long time, they will have to sit down for a time and apologize to one another in detail. This does not mean that every instance of sin must be mentioned by name, but it does mean that every area of sin must be addressed. For example, if a man has been lusting after other women for years, he does not have to say to his wife, "And then there was that time in 1988. . . ." But he must confess to her his mental infidelity and ask her to accept his apology.

If a couple maintains their fellowship with God, they will consequently do the same with one another. "But if we walk in the light as He is in the light, *we have fellowship with one another*, and the blood of Jesus Christ His Son cleanses us from all sin" (1 John 1:7). When a couple is in fellowship with one another, there is, in principle, no problem too great for them to work through together. It is therefore necessary to keep the marriage free of those sins which are hindrances to fellowship.

When sin has not been confessed in the home, fellowship is hindered. The Bible says that Christians are to confess their trespasses to one another (Jas. 5:16). If someone has a gift at the altar and remembers that his brother has something against him, he is to go and make it right (Matt. 5:23–24). This is always required, but we should immediately see how much more important it is to live this way *within the home*. Sin disrupts relationships. Sin never "blows over." If the mere passage of time could deal with the problem of sin, the Son of God died for no reason. Christian men must confess their sins to their wives. Christian women must confess their sins to their husbands.

If sin has not been forgiven in the home, fellowship is also hindered. The problem with confessing sins is that sometimes the other person can get angry over the sin revealed in the confession, or, if they already knew about it, they can still resentfully refuse to forgive. Before there was only one sin; now there are two. "And forgive us our debts, as we forgive our debtors" (Matt. 6:12). When husband and wife harbor resentment, they are preventing marital fellowship. It does not matter what the other person did, the one offended still has *no right to an unforgiving attitude*.

Another important aspect of this is the fact that when sin is not confessed and forgiven *immediately*, fellowship is hindered. God tells us to confess, and to forgive. He tells us to do both these things *now*. It is interesting to note that God never tells us to do the right thing tomorrow, or on Sunday, or after we get counseling, or have gone through twelve steps. We must always do the right thing *now*. We may be resolved to do the right thing toward our spouse later, but in the meantime, our fellowship is hindered, and other sins will come in like a flood. When we put off confession, the result is always more sin to confess. There is no good reason to procrastinate.

Wives must be careful not to try to usurp spiritual leadership in this. The Bible says, "Therefore, just as the church is subject to Christ, so let the wives be to their own husbands *in everything*" (Eph. 5:24). Wives are to be subject to their husbands in this as well. Pushing a man to become the spiritual leader will not make him one. He may not be much of a leader, but he is enough of one not to be led into leadership by a woman. Obviously, this does not mean the husband has the right to continue his abdication. When a man just sits there like a spiritual dead weight, fellowship is hindered. Husbands have a responsibility to "nourish and cherish" their wives (Eph. 5:29), and staring at the Idiot Box until it is time for sex is not one of God's appointed means for doing so.

Part of the problem for many couples is that they have trouble agreeing on what the problem is. The wife can think there is something wrong with everything, while the husband thinks there are just a few problems with some things. But in either case, the marriage really has a bad case of unconfessed sin. Our generation has witnessed a tremendous amount of marriage counseling and "help" for troubled relationships. It is not too much to say that marriage counseling is now an industry. But in this industry, precious little is said about *sin*. Everything can sound pretty good, but it is all a little blurry around the edges. Feel-good-about-yourself counsel does not help out at home where it counts. A problem marriage does not exhibit the symptoms of disease; it is not a syndrome; it is simply old-fashioned self-centeredness.

When a couple is serious about addressing the problem, they acknowledge their sin to God *as sin*, and thank Him for His forgiveness. If the sin has harmed anyone else, then restitution is necessary. If a wife has yelled at her husband, then she must ask forgiveness. She may not excuse herself on account of all the things he did or did not do which provoked her. The same thing applies to the husband; he must confess his sins, not hers. Just as she must confess her sins, not his. Each person could confess the sins of the other all day, and their joy would not be restored. He must confess speaking to her harshly, lusting after other women, spending money irresponsibly, not exercising spiritual leadership, and spending too much time in front of the television. She must confess having a critical and nagging spirit, showing disrespect to him in public, the absence of respect and obedience in the home, and all her attempts to be the spiritual leader in the home.

The one who is going to confess sin must sit down with a purpose to be specific before the Lord. Every instance should be lifted before God and called by the proper name. Lust is lust, malice is malice, and so forth. Where it has affected another person, the one apologizing must address his sin *only*. An apology ought not be a backhanded way of trying to get the other to apologize.

House Rules for Keeping Short Accounts

Confession of sin simply brings the account current. Early in our marriage, my wife and I determined to maintain certain house rules that would help us keep in step with one another. They were designed to help us keep short accounts. The rules applied whenever we had what we called a "bump."

The first rule we had was—*Never split up until things are resolved*. The husband and wife are to stay together. He doesn't go to work, she doesn't go shopping. They fix it *now*. This does not mean he will be late for work every day. A couple can get *in* fellowship as quickly as they got *out* of it. All it requires is an admittance of being in the wrong. If the "bump" was over the checkbook, it is not necessary to balance it before they go anywhere, but the sin must be confessed.

The second rule was—*Never let anyone into your home when there is no harmony there*. Do not let anyone into your home if you are not in fellowship. If a couple is in "mid-bump," and someone comes to the door, they shouldn't answer the door until they are back in fellowship. If it is raining, they should get back in fellowship *fast*.

The third rule is similar—*Never go anywhere else when you are out of fellowship*. If they have a bump on the way to church, they should fix it in the car before they go in to worship. If they have a bump on the way to a friend's house, they should not go in until things are right.

The fourth rule takes a little explanation. Many times a couple are with friends, and one of them says something which upsets the other one. If the sin was obvious to all, then the restitution should be made in the presence of all. Restitution should always be as public as the sin was. But many times, married couples can get out of fellowship with one another without the other people there knowing anything about it. The visible explosion happens in the car on the way home. When a problem happens around others, a couple should have a hand signal which means "I apologize," and an answer which means "Apology accepted." The rule is—*Never wait until later to fix things, even when you are surrounded by others.*

One more rule will help keep a man and his wife in step with the Lord and with one another. *Never have sexual relations when you are out of fellowship with one another.* This prevents turning what God intended as a unifying and wonderful experience into an act of hypocrisy.

Application of these rules will have a tremendous impact on a couple's relationship with their friends and family. Without such constraints, when a couple are having problems, all the friends and family know about it. But if these are put into practice, no one will *ever* see the couple, whether together or individually, when there is not harmony. God wants the man and woman to function as one in the world, and this kind of action will enable them to do so. It is not hypocrisy, because they really are in fellowship. They still do their laundry, but not in the front yard. And a strict adherence to these rules help to keep a sin problem from accumulating.

CHAPTER SIX

Miscellaneous Temptations

The Nice Guy Syndrome

Susan believes that the man she married is a very nice man, and so she does not really know why she is so frustrated with him. When she gets angry with him, she feels guilty—not because of the anger, but because it has no apparent cause. She is deeply dissatisfied, and yet feels that no one could really understand why she is frustrated. How can others understand, when *she* does not understand? Why is she so upset with such a nice guy?

In the Christian world today, countless marriages have not really been spiritually consummated. The marriage covenant has been made, and there has been physical consummation, but the marriage is still not right. It is not right because a marriage cannot be spiritually consummated if the husband acts the part of a spiritual eunuch. Such a eunuch is one who is impotent in his masculinity—as distinguished from his maleness, which is simply biological.

When a husband has this problem, the result for the wife is a temptation to deep-seated frustration and resentment. When she gives way to the temptation, the symptoms of this frustration can manifest themselves in many ways, both small and great. Some of the greater manifestations can include gluttony and drunkenness.

The irony is that such spiritual eunuchs are almost always nice guys. And because the symptoms of this spiritual neglect overtly appear in the wife, the watching world usually wonders "what on earth got into *her*?" As a consequence, she feels even greater frustration and resentment. There are more than enough examples of this pattern to give it a name—the Nice Guy Syndrome.

Now of course it is important to qualify this. Not all husbands with troubled wives are "nice guys." The Bible warns men not to be hard on their wives (Col. 3:19). But this Harsh Guy Syndrome is not hard to identify; when a woman has a man who treats her like dirt, there is no mystery as to why she is unhappy. The purpose here is to address those situations where a woman is thoroughly frustrated in a marriage with a *nice* man—and is consequently confused.

Countless nice Christian men have wives in this state of continual frustration. And the more frustrated the wife gets, the nicer the husband tries to be. Unfortunately, this "niceness" is not biblical gentleness. It is not the love discussed above; it is abdication, or "wimping out." From time to time, the situation gets to be too much, even for him, and he loses his temper over her frustration. But he knows that *that* is wrong, and so he apologizes, and goes back to his old pattern of indulging his wife, instead of loving her through leadership.

As Peter teaches, women need to understand they are being led by a *lord*. "As Sarah obeyed Abraham, calling him lord, whose daughters you are if you do good and are not afraid with any terror" (1 Peter 3:6). Unfortunately, many women are led (if it can be called leading) by men who believe themselves to be nothing more than walking, talking, living, breathing impositions. How many Christian women today can be considered as daughters of Abraham? How many of them could imagine calling their husband *lord* with a straight face? *Him?* But a *husband* is one who cultivates with authority.

Now it goes without saying that this authority must be exercised by a man with a Christ-like disposition to service. He must not wield his authority in a self-seeking way.

But he must wield it; he is a *husband*. It is tragic that in our culture the word husband is understood as nothing more than a male legally tied (for a few years) to a particular female. But as the etymology of the word should indicate, much more is involved. *Husbandry* is careful management of resources—it is stewardship. And when someone undertakes to husband a woman, he must understand that it cannot be done unless he acts with authority.

He must act as though he has a right to be where he is. He is the lord of the garden, and he has been commanded by God to see to it that this garden bears much fruit. This cannot be accomplished by "hanging around" in the garden and being nice. The garden must be managed, and ruled, and kept, and tilled. For many husbands, this is an alien concept; they certainly spend all their time in the garden, helping themselves to whatever fruit *happens* to grow, but they always have the furtive look of someone guilty of criminal trespass.

If someone wants a garden full of weeds, no husbandry is necessary. And if someone wants a wife full of frustration, nothing needs to be done to accomplish that either. All a man has to do is leave her alone. And nice guys are very good at leaving their wives alone.

A harsh man goes into the garden to trample underfoot. He is a destructive presence. There are men, tragically, who fit this description. But in the Christian church today, far more have the opposite problem. They do not do anything destructive *directly*, but they do stand around and watch the weeds grow. They are unsure of their right to be there, and pulling up weeds means that they have assumed responsibility for the state of the garden—he had better not do *that*. Such abdication is an abdication of *stewardship*; it is an abdication of *husbandry*. And the wife is frustrated because she has a husband in name, but she does not have a husband.

Some men may object by saying that their wives demand to be left alone. All they are doing is respecting their wives' wishes. There are two responses to this. One is that whether or not the wife has demanded to be left alone does not alter the fact that Christ has demanded that she *not* be left alone. "Husbands, love your wives, just as Christ also loved the church and gave Himself for it" (Eph. 5:25). The head of the woman is man, and the head of the man is Christ. And Christ has commanded husbands to imitate Him—and this necessitates a love which does not walk away, or stand by. Second, wives need to be led with a firm hand. They will often test their husbands in some area, and be deeply disappointed (and frustrated) if he gives in to her. It is crucial that a husband give to his wife what the Bible says she needs, rather than what she says she needs.

So a godly husband is a godly lord. A woman who understands this biblical truth and calls a certain man her *husband* is also calling him her *lord*. It is tragic that wholesale abdication on the part of modern men has made the idea of lordship in the home such a laughable thing. A man cannot get by with good intentions. He cannot get by with a pleasant demeanor. He cannot get by with a sweet disposition. He cannot get by on the good reputation he has in the church or in the neighborhood for being such a fine fellow. In a world of spiritual eunuchs, it is good to find a man who is more than simply male.

So this is the nature of the problem; many Christian men are nice guys, but they do not provide the strength of leadership that God requires and their wives need. "But I want you to know that the head of every man is Christ, the head of woman is man, and the head of Christ is God" (1 Cor. 11:3).

But diagnosis of a problem is not the same thing as solving it. Many husbands can readily see that they abdicate in a way they should not, but they do not know precisely what to do. The first thing to do is confess the general problem to God *as sin*. God has established a certain form of government in the family and we have no authority to alter or modify what He has done. Whether the alteration was done deliberately out of rebellion, or simply out of weakness, does not matter. It must be confessed if it does not conform to the pattern God established.

The second thing is to identify specific areas of abdication. When they are identified, they must be confessed as sin as well. Some specific examples are given below, but they are just examples. By no means should this list be considered exhaustive.

• *When the wife asks for counsel:* There are many occasions when a wife is feeling distressed about some difficulty, and she comes to her husband and says, "What should I do?" An abdicating husband will tell her that he does not care and that she can do whatever she wants to do. But when a wife seeks counsel from her husband, *she should always receive counsel.* When she comes to her husband and asks for a decision, he should always *make* a decision.

When a woman has come to my wife for counsel and advice, one of the things my wife commonly asks is whether or not her husband knows and approves of her seeking this counsel. And when they are talking about whatever her concern happens to be, my wife will frequently ask what her husband says about this. She has regularly heard things like, "He told me the decision was up to me." And this sort of abdication is not limited to trivial things—it has included life-changing questions, such as the use of birth control.

• *I tried that once:* Husbands who abdicate may defend themselves this way: "My wife did this once. She came to me for a decision, and I did make a decision. But then she resisted the decision. I concluded that she did not really want my decision so I let it go." This is an easy mistake to make, but it is a mistake nonetheless. The wife in this situation does not need him to make a decision; she needs him to make a *firm decision.*

Many times wives want their husbands to assume leadership in the home. So they ask for a decision, and the husband makes a decision. But then the wife wonders to herself whether this is a decision that the husband *really* is com-

mitted to, or whether he made it just to get her to be quiet
about it. And so she resists the decision. This is not because she rejects his leadership, but rather because she wants
to ensure that he is exercising *real leadership*. If he then
caves in, it is clear to her that he did not really make a
decision at all.

• *I told you so:* Suppose a decision has to be made, and
the husband and wife hold different opinions. After discussion, the husband abdicates, and they do what the wife
wanted to do. Suppose further that everything goes wrong
as a consequence. The husband's abdication can be seen
in his response to the disaster. If he says (or thinks), "Look
what doing it 'your way' did," then it shows he has abdicated leadership.

Now a godly husband may decide, after taking his wife's
concerns into account, to do things "her way." But in a godly
home, as soon as he does this, *it becomes his decision*. He
is entirely responsible for it. Once the decision is made,
it is his decision. If his wife tries to blame herself for how
it all turned out, he should restrain her—"No, dear. This
is all my doing." It may have been her idea in the discussion, but in a biblical home, it was his idea to *do* it.

• *Doing his own thing:* Some abdicating husbands may
think they are being decisive when they go off and do something without consulting with their wives at all. "You bought
what?" This sort of thing is a far cry from biblical leadership; if he thinks something is right to do, a godly husband
does not shy away from discussing it with his wife *before
he does it.* When a husband acts without consulting his wife,
it is commonly because he recognizes that she has practical veto power in the home. Because this particular thing
is something he really wants to do, he does it without letting her know beforehand. This is not leadership; it is self-
centered abdication.

How can a man break out of this pattern? We have already stated the importance of confessing the problem *as
sin*. So long as the problem is attributed to nothing more

than personality differences or sloughed off on different cultural backgrounds between husband and wife, the problem will remain. But a man who has not been the head of his home must confess his abdication as sin—he must treat it the same way he would treat theft, or adultery. It is disobedience.

Having confessed all known sin associated with the problem, the next step is to analyze and pray over the problem. A concerned husband should make a list with two categories.

The first category should contain a list of all the areas where things happen in the home *contrary* to the husband's expressed desires. For example, suppose he has said, on a number of occasions, that he thinks that the kids should not watch television. They watch television anyway, so he should put that on the list. If he thinks his wife should not ask her father for so much advice, but she persists, then he should put that on the list. He is listing those areas where his decisions are disregarded.

The second category should be a list of those areas where behavior in the home goes on because of the *absence* of leadership on his part. Suppose the wife sets the discipline standards for the kids. But suppose that she does so against her wishes—she has repeatedly asked him for guidance, and he has only said, "I don't know. You seem to be doing fine." Suppose she has asked for time in the Word together, but he never seems to get around to it. He should put that on the list.

As he puts this list together, he should be thorough. The first category will contain those areas of family life where his headship is ignored. The second category will list all those areas where his headship was never exercised. As he thinks over his list, he should be reminded again of his need for forgiveness. He should thank God for His graciousness to sinners, and rest in the fact that God has granted to us the perfect righteousness of His Son.

It is important that he not let his list become a com-

plaint list against his wife. The point is not to get out of
the sin of abdication and into the sin of bitterness and resentment. The husband is the one who abdicated, and he
is now merely identifying those specific areas which need
to be corrected.

When he has completed the list, he should pray over
it for several days. During this time, he may find himself
adding or deleting things. Taking the time to do this will
prevent a hasty or ill-advised confrontation with his wife.
When he feels confident that the list accurately describes
the problem, he should sit down and have a talk with his
wife. He will probably need to set aside several hours in
order to discuss the problem with her thoroughly. If there
are older children (teenagers), it may be necessary to sit
down with them in a similar sort of way.

He should tell his wife that he has confessed his sin of
abdication to God, and that he wants to ask her forgiveness as well. *He must not attack or blame her.* His demeanor
should be one of humility. He has wronged her, and is now
making restitution. If she has sinned in this (as she probably has), he is not yet qualified to serve as one who cor-
rects (Gal. 6:1).

They should go over the list together. The most important part is the category where decisions or attempts
at leadership were ignored, and the husband did not do anything about it. He should ask for her forgiveness, and for
her help as he seeks to confront the sin. When they are
done, they should pray together.

After doing this, the chances are that both husband and
wife will both feel a lot better. But the problem is not yet
resolved. Sometime within the next week, the husband should
pick one of the relatively minor areas on the list where there
has been a problem. He should make a decision in this problem area. If the old pattern of disregarding him begins to
manifest itself, he should draw his wife aside and remind
her that he does not want to fall into his old habit of abdication. Regardless of what happens, he must *not* change his

decision. If his wife gets upset, he must not back off. If she explains that *this* situation is different because . . . he must not back off. This is crucial.

Obviously, he should spend enough time in preparation and prayer over this decision to ensure that he does not make a decision that is foolish or self-centered. But even if his choice was not the best one he could have made, the *issue* is not the issue. What is at stake is a recovery of godly leadership in the home.

The reason he should start with a relatively minor issue is simple. If one were to begin lifting weights, he would not begin by putting all the weights in the weight room on the bar. If one were to begin jogging, he does not start by running ten miles. This sort of thing guarantees failure, and discourages future attempts. It is the same with this. The husband is simply breaking a bad habit. This will be difficult enough without all the additional complications that come with a big decision. Consequently, he should start with the issue of what restaurant to visit that evening, and not whether to sell the house and move to the Yukon.

And when he has successfully made one decision stick, *he must make another one.* He is learning how to walk in leadership, and he will soon discover it is like all forms of walking—one foot at a time.

Differences Between Men and Women

We live in an egalitarian culture which hates "unfair" distinctions of any kind. While this position may seem obvious to the modern mind, it is thoroughly unbiblical. If God has created us with certain differences and distinctions, and He did, we ignore those distinctions at our peril. This is particularly the case when it comes to the differences between men and women.

But when we make distinctions about classes of people, we must generalize. Therefore, we should justify the legitimacy of some forms of generalizing. In Titus 1:12, Paul states the following: "One of them, a prophet of their own, said, 'Cretans are always liars, evil beasts, lazy gluttons.'" Here Paul is generalizing by saying Cretans are always liars, evil brutes, lazy gluttons. Paul feels free to make a generalization even though it is not true in each and every instance. One of their *own* prophets was obviously not always a liar, because what he said here is true. This particular prophet is an exception to the rule, but the generalization remains legitimate.

When we make sober generalizations we are not being irrational. We may look at the world and observe that different kinds of people tend to follow certain patterns of behavior. Having made the observation, we can then seek to understand which differences come from God and which differences are sinful and need to be changed. The distinctive features of the Cretans mentioned by Paul were sinful, and Paul was writing so that Titus would conduct his ministry with a view to changing them.

We can also generalize about men and women, husbands and wives. For example, men are taller than women (and no, not always). Nevertheless, the generalization is legitimate. We should simply understand and enjoy certain God-given differences between men and women. Other differences, however, tend to produce sinful responses to one another.

Some of the differences relate to the roles that God assigned to men and women. For example, a hammer and a crescent wrench differ, but the differences are not arbitrary. Someone invented both the hammer and the crescent wrench, each for a particular purpose. The differences between them are design-feature differences. In a similar way, the different tasks assigned to both men and women will account for many of the differences. Such differences can be manifested in many ways.

For example, suppose a husband comes home from work, and it occurs (even) to him that quite possibly his wife did not have the best day. He asks her if anything is wrong. She says *nothing* is wrong. By this she means that so many things are wrong that she cannot put her finger on one thing alone, and besides, *anybody* could see that something was wrong. He says, "Good. For a second there I thought something was wrong," and goes out to watch the news. Later in the evening, of course, he discovers his error—there is a big blow-up. She thinks he should have picked up on the fact that something was wrong, and he maintains that he *asked*, and she said *nothing* was wrong. Men and women have different ways in which they use the English language. When we fail to properly translate our words and thoughts, problems follow on hard.

As discussed elsewhere, men and women are *oriented* differently (1 Cor. 11:9). But one of the fundamental ways we express our orientation is through language. If couples do not allow for differing applications of English, then they will have real trouble communicating. If they allow for it, and come to understand it, they can enjoy their differences. If they do not, such differences will be a real source of temptation. Misunderstanding of what the other is trying to say invites the sin of imputing motives. But when we sinfully impute motives, we hinder our fellowship. The Bible says that love "bears all things, believes all things, hopes all things, endures all things" (1 Cor. 13:7). Love does *not* jump to conclusions, and it does not try to read the motives of the other person's heart. Whenever there has been any kind of conflict, it is very easy to be wrong about the other person's motives, and very difficult to be right about them.

Men and women also *think* differently. There are times when a wife is distraught over something, and the husband thinks he should lecture her on why it all happened the way it did. But his gifts of analysis, however sharp, are no good in that situation. At that point, she does not need information—*she needs a hug*. He should tell her that everything will be all right, and he should then keep his mouth shut. This does not mean that his analytic abilities have no use. If he comes to her later, and tells her that he has been thinking and praying about what happened yesterday and that he has some thoughts on how to deal with it the next time, she will be very appreciative.

Differences in thinking are apparent elsewhere. Women appear to have multi-track minds and can skip from one track to another without missing anything. Men appear to have linear, one-track minds. One time my wife and I were out driving and looking at houses, and we saw one we were interested in, and talked about it for a bit. Three days later Nancy resumed our conversation where we had left off without any antecedent at all; needless to say I did not know what we were talking about. At the same time, it is uncanny how women can get together and speak in this way to one another without anyone getting lost. Women are much more flexible in how they can relate one thing to another. In their minds everything is connected. With men, it is much easier to disconnect one subject from another subject. Consequently, if something is bothering a woman in one area, it is much easier for it to surface in a completely different area. The man is baffled because he is trying to figure out how they got from one subject to the other.

Because of this, women should take care that this sort of thing does not build up over three months' time and then explode. As soon as she resists temptation to sin in a particular area, she should make a mental note to talk to her husband about this at the first appropriate time. If *sin* occurs and it shows up as an attitude problem (someone gets a bit frosty), then the apologies need to be made immediately. If *temptation* occurs, it should be put off and addressed at the first possible opportunity for good to be done.

Also, many women want their husbands to do little thoughtful things *spontaneously* and not because anyone taught them to do so. Take the example of a husband buying his wife flowers—men will not do such things spontaneously. If it appears to be spontaneous, then it simply means that he was taught well and taught early. If a son is brought up correctly and is taught by his father to do such things for his mother, by the time he gets married it will be spontaneous *for him*. He should seek to learn *spontaneity*, and she should learn to let him *learn* it.

Abdication and Debt

> Neither a borrower, nor a lender be;
> For loan oft loses both itself and friend,
> *And borrowing dulls the edge of husbandry . . .*
>   Shakespeare

Although God has established the man as the *husband* of the family, many Christian men have, in the wedding ceremony, assumed the label without assuming the corresponding responsibilities and duties.

God has created us *male and female*; consequently, such abdication on the part of men runs contrary to the way we are created. As a result, disobedience of this nature in the home generates a fundamental and deep-seated guilt on the part of the husband. Now when men feel guilty for something, and they do not seek the Lord in repentance, they will always seek for a way to atone for their guilt on their own. If they do not consciously trust in Christ's payment for sin, the natural reaction is to look for some way to make the payment themselves. Apart from faith in the Guilt Offering, men will invent and multiply various other guilt offerings. These alternative guilt offerings are commonly financial, and in a world of easy credit, it is easy for an abdicating husband to get into serious financial trouble.

The problem is two-fold. First, husbands who have abdicated generally will also have a tendency to abdicate when it comes to setting financial limits for their households. They consequently allow their wives to spend beyond the family's resources; this is a subset of the larger problem of abdication. Because the husband is afraid to say *no* on any issue, it makes sense when we see that he cannot say *no* on financial issues.

But the second aspect of this problem is even more serious. Husbands can often *encourage* their wives to spend beyond the family's resources. This encouragement is the result of the husband trying to palliate his guilt. When the husband is not providing for his wife's spiritual need for strong leadership, he can fall for the easy alternative of giving her *things* instead. The result is that guilty husbands, in this world of easy credit, are allowed the illusionary belief that they are far better providers than they actually are.

When an abdicating husband gives his wife the credit card, and sends her off to shop beyond their means, her purchases are a fitting symbol of her relationship with her husband—provision from the void. But for whatever reason, when goods are purchased with non-existent funds, there is quite possibly larceny in the heart. Nevertheless, God still rules the world; thieves and rascals will come to slavery. It remains true that we reap what we sow.

The Bible teaches that the borrower becomes a slave to the lender (Prov. 22:7), and that Christians should not willingly become slaves (1 Cor. 7:23). Many men have come to this position of servitude outside the home because they had already come to that same position *within the home.*

Godly husbands indeed serve their wives, but they do so with the authority of love and self-sacrifice. A true husband is one who gives himself away to his wife and family *with authority.* Our Lord Jesus had this servant's heart, but it did not remove His authority; it was the foundation of it. The servitude which comes from abdication is something else entirely.

Exercising responsibility as the head of a family takes diligence, work, and courage. The Bible teaches that doing a responsible job of leading in the home is a prerequisite for leadership in the church: ". . . if a man does not know how to rule his own house, how will he take care of the church of God?" (1 Tim. 3:5). Just as responsibility in the home prepares a man for responsibility elsewhere, so irresponsibility in the home will lead to irresponsibility outside—in this case to creditors.

We must solve the problem at the source. It is all too easy to lament the bills—as though they were a result of some astrological phenomenon. But they are not; they are the result of spending too much. And in the situation we have been discussing, too much *money* is spent because too little *diligence* is spent in husbandry. As with all sin, the solution is repentance before God and acknowledgment of that repentance to those who have been affected by the sin. In this case, a husband should confess his abdication to God *as sin* and should have a long talk with his wife about how he has failed to be a true husband to her. But this, by itself, is not sufficient.

A husband will see no lasting change unless the husband sets himself to be a student of the Word of God—all of it. Many turn the pages of the Bible as though they were going through a cafeteria line. But our responsibility is to be instructed in the *whole* counsel of God (Acts 20:27). For heads of households, this study must certainly include the subject of debt and finances. But many Christians reply that they want biblical solutions to their problems, but that they do not have the time to study the Bible. This is rebellious nonsense. All of us, in every station of life, must live and die by the Word.

Pornography

One of the principal problems with pornography is the damage it has caused through its lies about sexuality. The central lie in pornography is that it says men and women have different bodies but the same kind of brains. It says that women are as eager for sex and approach sex in the same way that men do. This is the central lie of pornography. In *The Four Loves*, C.S. Lewis said that when a man, in the grip of lust, says he wants a woman, that is really the *last* thing he wants. He does *not* want a woman, but rather a particular sensation for which a woman is the necessary apparatus. If he really wanted a woman, then he would also want a house, a picket fence, curtains, three kids, and the rest of his life with this particular woman. The man under the control of lust simply wants a sexual partner who is willing to pretend that she is not mentally and emotionally a woman. For example, a prostitute is obviously acting as a female, but she has to deny her womanhood. For whatever reason, she is willing to pretend that she is not a woman on the inside.

If we interviewed a thousand men who were promiscuous, we would find we had a thousand men with a lack of self-control with regard to sexual temptation. If we were to do the same with a thousand promiscuous women, we would not find a thousand women with a sexual problem, but rather with a security problem. They are generally not looking for great sexual satisfaction, but rather for emotional security.

When I was a small boy, our family visited some friends of my parents. When we were driving home, my father mentioned to my mother that their friends were going to have serious problems when their daughter grew older—problems with men. He said this because as soon as he sat down in their home, their young daughter was all over him. Sadly, his prophecy was fulfilled. If a strange man comes into a home, and a little girl climbs on his lap, something is seriously wrong. The girl has a big vacuum in her life—a need for masculine attention—that is not being filled by her father. She has a hunger for masculine attention; when she enters adolescence, she will suddenly discover that she now has a commodity with which she can bargain, and she will be tempted to begin to use it. This is because she still has a need for the security, and a void that still needs to be filled with masculine attention. Now all of a sudden men are *voluntarily* paying attention to her. Before, as a little girl, she was a nuisance chasing after men, and now they are coming to her. Of course they are after one thing, and she is after another. They consequently make an exchange that makes neither one of them truly happy.

Criticism

In marital conversation, words like "never" and "always" are attack words. Suppose the wife tells her husband that she feels like she is running the home by herself while he just sits there and reads the paper. If she just lets him have it, then they are going to have a fight. But if she expresses her concerns without accusing words like *always* and *never*, he will be in a much better position to respond in a godly way. The Bible requires us to be quick to listen, and slow to speak. In this example, if the husband does this, he is already three-fourths of the way toward diffusing a potentially dangerous situation.

Most of us need practice in being quick to listen. Suppose the wife presents her concern, and she does it without anger. If he responds by defending himself (whether he is right or wrong does not matter), then he is probably not being quick to listen. But if he hears her out, and then says something like this—"Let me make sure I am understanding you. You think that. . . ." After that point, however he responds, she at least knows that he heard and understood her. This is obedience to the command to be *fast* in listening.

Listening in this way has two advantages. The first advantage is that it helps in diffusing a potential problem. It is hard to fight with someone who is listening to you considerately. Second, whenever it is done, it is difficult for the other person to slip into a "never" sort of statement such as, "You never listen to what I have to say."

Husbands and wives have trouble understanding one another for the same reason other people do—they do not *listen* to one another. "So then, my beloved brethren, let every man be swift to hear, slow to speak, slow to wrath"

(James 1:19). The Bible requires us to place a good deal of importance on *listening*. A good way to discipline one's self in this is to repeat back what the other has said. This ensures that they understand that you were listening. This is particularly important for men to do because they are generally much poorer in communicating with their wives than they ought to be. Women are much more interested in communication with husbands, and are usually better at it than men, although they have problems with it too. For all their vaunted skills in analysis, men frequently do not understand what a woman is saying. It might take two or three times of repeating back what she has said before she says, "Yes, that's right."

When someone offers a criticism, it is difficult to be quick to listen and slow to speak. The one with the criticism will often want an immediate response; it is usually not wise to offer one because the response will tend to be defensive and not objective. Suppose the wife has a basic concern about disciplining the children ("I feel as though I am rearing them by myself"). She expresses this to her husband, and then he repeats back to her what she has said. Now he is either guilty or innocent. If he is guilty, then the Lord may speak to his conscience right away—he should admit the problem right away. But if he is innocent, he should not maintain his innocence on the spot. He should instead be slow to respond and slow to defend himself.

But if the husband has a reasonable defense, the last thing he should do is to present it at this moment. He should show that he understands what her concerns are, repeat each one of them, and then say he would like to talk about the issue later. He needs some time to think it over and pray about it. That means if he concludes that his wife is wrong, he is to do so thoughtfully and prayerfully, after a period of time. If it is obvious that she is right, it should be admitted immediately. A quarrel is diffused in either way.

The goal is not to win the argument, but to maintain the relationship. When the husband is ahead 15–3 in husband/wife fights, they are both losers. But if the quarrels are diffused, chances are good that both will come to realize the legitimacy of both masculine and feminine perspectives and that the balance is to be found somewhere in the middle.

Newlyweds often think that being close and intimate with one another means sharing everything that happens to come into their heads, including their temptations. There is no finer way to chase your tail than to share your temptations with one another. If one is tempted to sin, and confesses it to the other person, then that presents a temptation to *them*. There is no sin in being tempted. It is not necessary to apologize for any thought that happens to come into one's head. If husbands and wives get on the treadmill of confessing temptations, they will embark on a merry chase indeed.

At the same time, someone may share a temptation if the other person is not currently in the middle of causing it. Suppose every time the husband drops his socks in the middle of the living room, the wife is tempted. If he has just done so, and his wife sees it, then that is not the time to say anything. However, the wife may take a different course. When it has not just happened, she could say to him, "Honey, could I talk to you about something that is a temptation to me?" He then gives permission, which means that he *asked* for her input. She then says, "This is not a temptation to me right now, but it is a concern to me." There is no better way to turn a temptation into a sin than to share the temptation in the middle of the temptation.

Jealousy

Christian husbands are to imitate the Lord's love for His people in their treatment of their wives. We are of course to do so in all respects. But this imitation will not always be predictable. Sometimes it will lead us in ways we may not have expected.

"For you shall worship no other god, for the Lord, whose name is Jealous, is a jealous God . . ." (Ex. 34:14). The Lord we serve is *named* Jealous; not only does He expect His people to abstain from spiritual adultery, He also requires that they refrain from "mild" flirtations and dalliances as well. He has no tolerance for infidelity in any of its forms. He is *jealous*.

The apostle Paul uses the picture of jealousy in the context of human marriage as an image for the church. "For I am jealous for you with godly jealousy. For I have betrothed you to one husband, that I may present you as a chaste virgin to Christ" (2 Cor. 11:2). The picture is a noble one; it does not conjure up images of a green-gilled apostle skulking around in an unreasonable attempt to "control" or "manipulate" the Corinthians.

We can easily test ourselves to see whether we understand the positive value of jealousy. Suppose a young man was engaged to marry a young woman, and he discovered that she was not a virgin. This was important to him, and so after prayerful consideration, he broke off the engagement. If our attitude is, "What a jerk!" or "I'll bet *he's* not a virgin!" or anything else comparable, we have a serious problem. We have fallen into the trap of thinking that while virginity is a good thing, this does not necessarily mean non-virginity is a bad thing.

Now of course, the young man is not *required* to break the engagement. But if he does so, and if we all begin flinging things at *him*, we are simply demonstrating that we do not understand why the Bible describes Joseph as a righteous man (Matt. 1:19).

Now of course, the virtue of jealousy can go off the rails just like anything else. Love can cease to be love through indulgence. Leadership can cease to be leadership through tyranny. Work can cease to be work through busyness. This is a fallen world, and everything can be corrupted, including the godly necessity of jealousy.

So how can jealousy go to seed? Let's return to our

example of the young man given earlier. Suppose he decided that he did want to marry the young lady, and so they married. Suppose further that her earlier sexual history did not bother him during the engagement, but shortly after the marriage, he became consumed with the subject of her previous fornication. He wants names, he wants details, he wants to know her attitudes toward *him*, and so forth. He pesters her constantly for details, and, to use Churchill's description of a fanatic, he can't change his mind, and he won't change the subject.

Our temptation could be to write him off as hopeless. This is not because our world has a high view of forgiveness, but rather a manifestly low view of sin. We must fix it in our minds that the husband's problem is *not* that he takes her previous sin seriously. That, in itself, is good. His problem is that he takes himself too seriously. The sin was in the past, before he was her husband, and the only one who can deal with the past is our Lord and Savior Jesus Christ. Husbands are not equipped to protect their wives from the past. *Only God can forgive sin.*

The irony is that in seeking to protect her from the past (which he cannot do), he is leaving her unprotected in the present. Godly jealousy in a husband seeks to protect the woman *now*. But the only protection such a wife needs right now is from her unreasonable husband. Retroactive jealousy is therefore bad, not because there is jealousy involved, but rather because a finite man is trying to fix something beyond his power to fix. As a result, his poor wife is left in a position of profound insecurity. In contrast, godly jealousy provides security. It is constructive—because it guards and protects someone greatly in need of such protection.

Biblical jealousy helps us to understand the value of submission. The Bible teaches that a wife must be submissive to her own husband. It does not teach that a woman must be submissive to men generally. It is true that when wives are submissive to their own husbands, this will be obvious

on the broader cultural level, both in civil and ecclesiasti-
cal society. But one of the most obvious things about the
Bible's teaching is that submission to a man *excludes* submission to other men. Christ taught us that no man can
have two masters; the same truth applies to women. Submission to a particular man means non-submission to countless other particular men.

So when a man is jealous of his wife in the biblical way,
he is protecting her from submission to other men. When
a father is jealous for his daughter's purity, he watches out
for her interests. And when such a father gives his daughter in marriage to a man worthy of the position, the new
husband promises the father that he will be equally jealous. So when a godly woman submits to her husband, she
is being liberated through godly male protection.

The fact that this truth enrages feminists should not
distress us at all. Women are *inescapably* in need of such
protection; the only difference between feminists and Christians is that Christians place the duty of protection with
fathers and husbands while feminists place the duty of protection with various male-dominated federal agencies. The
lesson should be clear. Christian men are called to cultivate the biblical virtue of jealousy.

CHAPTER SEVEN

The Marriage Bed is Honorable

On Alert

In writing about human sexual practices it is perilously easy
to be tasteless, unbiblical, or just plain wrong. Christians
who read such material need always to be alert—even when
it is written by Christians. Christians have an unhappy tendency to assume that anything that comes from an evangelical publishing house must be biblically sound. Tragically, this is far from true.

Often Christians do a poor job teaching on this subject (whether in sermons, books, seminars, etc.) because
they are following the world, with some sort of respect-
able time-lag of about five to ten years. When the world
claims "progress" in a particular area, often Christians go
along, while keeping a decent distance behind. And of
course, one major area where observers have claimed much
"progress" is with regard to our sexual behavior. We have
been liberated from the older prudishness and have come
to rejoice in the new "openness."

In this area, the world does not hesitate to teach. Humanistic doctrines become current and gradually find their
way into the church. Because the church does not teach
scripturally on the subject, Christians adopt a humanistic
perspective by default. When the church *does* get around
to teaching on sex, we find that the teaching is an echo of
the world's thinking than an answer to it.

Consequently, many people resist any attempt to discuss sexual behavior biblically. Its discipline will offend many, and its freedom will offend the rest. What follows here is one such an attempt, made with the realization that it may be far too "restricting" for some and far too "liberal" for others. Nevertheless, we are required to live, and love, by *every word* that proceeds from the mouth of God. For Christians, it should not much matter if the Lord's instrument for bringing us this word was Solomon or Paul. They both taught what was from God, and their teaching is therefore fully consistent. For Christians who are tired of being battered by the radical lies of the world and the knee-jerk reactions of some Christians, the doctrine will perhaps be a relief.

The Will of God and Sexual Satisfaction

The Bible teaches that God wills the sexual purity of His people. "For this is the will of God, your sanctification: that you should abstain from sexual immorality; that each of you should know how to possess his own vessel in sanctification and honor, not in passion of lust, like the Gentiles who do not know God . . ." (1 Thess. 4:3–5). This expression of the will of God is one which many Christian men need to learn. Many have not learned how to take a wife in a pure and honorable way. They come to the marriage bed with the same kind of passionate lust which is characteristic of unbelievers. But Paul tells us here that Christians are to be different in *how* they love, not just in *whom* they love.

Modernity has sent us all off on a frustrating search for the perfect sexual experience, and this vain quest, this sexual snipe-hunt, has even ensnared many Christian married couples. We are told, and not just by non-Christians, that we have an obligation to have "dynamic sex-lives." But the subtle distortion here can have one of two results. It either leads to a frenzied hunt for the ultimate sexual experience, or it leads to an acquiescing frustration and dissatisfaction with "normal" sex. But the modern apostles of sexual pleasure who push this sort of dynamic pleasure as the *norm* have forgotten two related factors: one is the fact of emotional inflation and the other is our finitude.

First, if everything is special, then nothing is. If everything is "dynamic," then the dynamic becomes ordinary. They must continue to seek some new thrill in order to keep up with the "dynamic imperative." The law of diminishing returns takes hold and other novelties have to be tried simply to maintain the same level of excitement. This is because Christian men have not learned how to take a wife in a pure way; they do so with the passionate (and frustrated) lust of the nonbelievers. This frustrating search for the Perfect Orgasm Every Time has ensnared many Christian marriages. This distortion can easily lead to various perversions in the frenzy for more and more sexual pleasure. Now some readers may be scratching their heads at this point and wondering if this means that married couples should *not* enjoy "dynamic" sex. Of course they should—*sometimes*. But if everything must be "dynamic," then they must always seek some new thrill, usually involving a good deal of weirdness, in order to keep up with the "dynamic imperative."

The second problem with this approach is our finitude. We are finite creatures, and, consequently, our capacity for sexual pleasure has *set limits*. But lust, by its very nature, is incapable of recognizing such limits. Lust demands from a finite thing what only the infinite God can provide. Therefore, when someone in the grip of lust comes up against the wall of his finitude, he demands alternatives. This unwillingness to submit to the finitude of sexual pleasure has produced all manner of sexual perversions. Consequently, Paul tells us to guard the marriage bed against the philosophy of such lusters. Everything about sexual lust is futile and grasping after wind.

A man and woman who accept their finitude and who seek to honor God in how they love each other will of course enjoy themselves sexually. But that enjoyment will have the *normal range* that is to be expected from any physical pleasure. Sometimes they will enjoy a "steak dinner," and it really will be extraordinary. Other times it will be quite ordinary—macaroni and cheese—but still enjoyable. Should they enjoy extraordinary sexual experiences? Yes, of course—*sometimes*. But at no time should they accept the lie that sexual pleasure is subnormal unless it matches the standards set by humanistic sexual therapists. Christians should recognize that "scientists" with clipboards who watch other people have sex do not really have a firm grasp of what *normal* means.

This rebellion against our finitude is connected to a rebellion against the *biological* purpose of the sexual union, which is the procreation of children. Now recognizing this biological purpose does *not* mean that every sexual act must have in mind the purpose of begetting children, nor does it necessitate a prohibition of birth control. (A further discussion of birth control can be found in the next chapter.) But for our purposes here, it is important to resist the modern desire to establish a permanent and lasting divorce between the sexual union and the birth of children.

The biological purpose of food, which is to supply the body with needed energy, gives us a good point of comparison. This biological function of food could have been fulfilled without any regard for the enjoyments of taste. God could have made all food taste like cold oatmeal and yet be very nutritious. He did not, and we thank Him for it. But the pleasures of taste notwithstanding, the purpose of food is not exhausted simply because we have enjoyed certain pleasurable sensations in our mouths.

Frustration with finitude and a rebellion against biological limits, seeking to supply sex with a continual "high octane kick," will ultimately *destroy* sexual pleasure. My argument here is consequently a defense of sexual pleasure, not an attack on it. But it is a defense of sexual pleasure the way God gave it to us—a wonderful gift to His creatures. To push beyond such set boundaries is to destroy it.

Of course this understanding is subject to great distortions and misrepresentations. Many think that people who honor God's boundaries around the sexual relationship are blue-nosed prudes, incapable of having any fun themselves and who desire that no one else have a good time either. But suppose a Christian were talking with an unbelieving friend, and the subject of food came up. He asks the believer, "What do you think the purpose of eating is?" The Christian replies that the purpose of food is to supply the body with needed energy. The nonbeliever guffaws, "You fundamentalist sap! Are you trying to tell me that you don't enjoy eating?"

Of course he does. But why does he eat? Sometimes he eats because he is hungry, sometimes because his wife has prepared an attractive meal, and sometimes just because the food is there. But these reasons for eating are not the same as the reason for *food*. A man may have many different legitimate reasons for eating, but he must never rebel against and deny the biological purpose of food. If he does, then ultimately he will cease to enjoy the eating. If the pleasures of eating are divorced from the biological function of food, then the pleasures derived from eating will not last long. All created things cease to fulfill their potential if they are removed from the place God assigned to them. Eating disorders illustrate how people can be enslaved to a particular activity, and yet be simultaneously destroying their capacity to enjoy that activity.

In the same way, a Christian married couple may have any number of reasons for their lovemaking on any given occasion, ranging from simple sexual appetite to emotional comfort. But none of this changes the basic biological fact, which is the possibility of children, which is unaltered by the other purposes and benefits. The one who seeks to serve the pleasure *alone* is like a man who thinks the purpose of farming is to get a sun tan.

The Blessedness of the Marriage Bed

Having set a guard against the philosophy of lust, the biblical Christian must guard himself in the other direction as well. While sexual pleasure is threatened by the unbelievers who would stampede through it, it is also unfortunately threatened by "decent" people who, frankly, are afraid of it and run away in the other direction. But such a reaction against unabashed sexual pleasure must ignore the clear teaching of the Bible just as much as the former error does. The Christian marriage bed must be both disciplined *and* liberated. But the standards for *both* must come from the Scriptures and only from the Scriptures. We must not seek to be "liberated" by the world and its lust, and we must not be "disciplined" by vestigial Victorian prudishness in the church. Both are anti-scriptural.

We have already pointed out that we are finite creatures, and that this finitude affects our capacity for sexual pleasure. It *is* limited, whatever those who are dominated by lust may say or demand. But this is not to say that our capacity for sexual pleasure is *small*. The rejection of the frenzied pagan rush after a constant sexual high does not exclude a disciplined Christian cultivation of sexual enjoyment. It is at this point we may turn to the clear example set in the Song of Solomon.

In doing so, I am not intending to supply a commentary on the book as a whole. The purpose here is much more limited and seeks to answer one basic question. What do the images of the Song of Solomon indicate to us about sexual propriety in the marriage bed?

First, the obvious. The Song of Solomon is an erotic love poem. The purpose of looking at certain portions of it here is to help Christian couples who accept the boundaries of their finitude, but who also want to know exactly what those boundaries are. A careful reading of the book shows, almost at once, that the boundaries were not in any way established by Miss Grundy, but rather by the God who created sexual union. In some places, the meaning of the poet can hardly be missed, and for prudish Christians, the clarity of the point is all the more embarrassing. But embarrassment is not an appropriate response for Christians; all of Scripture is inspired, and is profitable for instruction.

In other places of the Song, the point is oblique enough to be the subject of debate. Nevertheless, even the fact that there is room for discussion is helpful. This is because the benefit to be gained from the Song is not a list of rules or techniques but rather an *attitude* toward lovemaking.

One of the first things to learn from the Song is the lawfulness of learning in this fashion. It is legitimate to read and learn from the *erotica* of the Song. This erotica is not graphic, or obscene, but it *is* clearly and unambiguously sexual. Put another way, the Bible contains literary passages, which we may read, in which another couple is engaged in passionate lovemaking. Nevertheless we are only invited to observe *through a veil*. Part of the reason the writing cannot be considered graphic (or pornographic) is related to a common problem which some have with interpreting the book. Readers of the Song commonly complain that it is difficult to keep all the characters straight. For example, is the woman's lover Solomon or someone else? But this ambiguity is very helpful. It would be inappropriate to invade the bedchamber of two individuals as individuals; what we have in the Song is a paradigmatic couple, setting an example which may be lawfully studied and observed—and imitated. But the imitation is not an imitation of various techniques, but an imitation of demeanor and attitude.

As a result of such imitation, we learn certain important aspects of biblical lovemaking. First, the lovemaking in the Song of Solomon is pervasively sensual, meaning that it involves far more than just the sense of touch. In the first three verses alone, two of the senses are named—taste and smell. "Let him kiss me with the kisses of his mouth—for your love is better than wine" (Song 1:2). The smell is that of sweet perfume: "Because of the fragrance of your good ointments, your name is ointment poured forth; therefore the virgins love you" (Song. 1:3). The fragrance is not just a generally pleasant atmosphere, it is very much a part of their coupling. "A bundle of myrrh is my beloved to me, that lies all night between my breasts" (Song 1:13).

This is why the general surroundings also matter. Not only should the lover be attractive, so should the surroundings be. The man and woman are not animals in heat; this is civilized lovemaking. "Behold, you are handsome, my beloved! Yes, pleasant! Also our bed is green. The beams of our houses are cedar, and our rafters of fir" (Song 1:16–17).

But the woman does not just say that her love is like tasting; she says that her lover is tasted. At the risk of be-laboring the obvious, this tasting does not occur with pursed lips. Neither the woman nor the man are drinking this wine through a straw. "Like an apple tree among the trees of the woods, so is my beloved among the sons. I sat down in his shade with great delight, and his fruit was sweet to my taste" (Song 2:3). The man knows the same pleasure in tasting her as well; he knows that her mouth is a well of delight. This is *biblical* kissing. "Your lips, O my spouse, drip as the honeycomb; honey and milk are under your tongue; and the fragrance of your garments is like the fragrance of Lebanon" (Song 4:11).

In the description of this book, the woman *is* a garden, and the woman also *has* a garden. First, we see that the woman is a garden. "A garden enclosed is my sister, my spouse, a spring shut up, a fountain sealed" (Song 4:12). But there is an inner garden within this garden. This is what he is drawn towards the most, and she is eager for him to come and enjoy himself fully. She invokes the wind to bring him there. "Awake, O north wind, and come, O south! Blow upon my garden, that its spices may flow out. Let my beloved come to his garden and eat its pleasant fruits" (Song 4:16). She obviously enjoys her lover as well.

In all of this we can see the superiority of the biblical

description of lovemaking. The liberated modern, with the furrowed brow of a frustrated technocrat, wants to talk about the various positions of sexual engineering, accompanied by charts, diagrams, and technical manuals—along with stern and graphic lectures to all of us repressed Puritans. But the biblical description of such things has the virtues of both clarity *and* propriety. Christians should both read the Song and read *into* it. If they do so, they do not need to borrow anything from the world.

The woman's lover is drawn to her entire body. "How beautiful are your feet in sandals, O prince's daughter! The curves of your thighs are like jewels, the work of the hands of a skillful workman. Your navel is a rounded goblet; it lacks no blended beverage. Your waist is a heap of wheat set about with lilies" (Song 7:1–2). It is obviously lawful for a godly husband to admire, kiss, taste, and caress his wife wherever he pleases.

He also speaks openly concerning his admiration for her. "Your two breasts are like two fawns, twins of a gazelle, which feed among the lilies" (Song 4:5; 7:3). He then compares her to a palm tree, and her breasts are like the clusters of the vine. He resolves to climb the tree in order to reach that fruit. He ascends her body in order to reach and taste the clusters. He comes to her mouth which has the fragrance of apples, and then tastes and drinks the wine which is there. The woman is clearly pleased to be such a tree, and for her mouth to be such a goblet, and rejoices in how smooth her wine is to his taste.

> This stature of yours is like a palm tree, and your breasts like its clusters. I said, 'I will go up to the palm tree, I will take hold of its branches.' Let now your breasts be like clusters of the vine, the fragrance of your breath like apples, and the roof of your mouth like the best wine.
>
> The Shulamite: The wine goes down smoothly for my beloved, moving gently the lips of sleepers (Song 7:7–9).

As Christian lovers, our enjoyment of lovemaking should be deep and lasting. The joy of sex, about which the world talks much and knows very little, is a gift to us from God. Because God is good to us, the man gives and receives, and the woman receives and gives, tremendous pleasure. "His left hand is under my head, and his right hand embraces me" (Song 2:6).

One Flesh

The sexual union is such an intimate aspect of our lives that it has to be protected if *we* are to be protected. It must have a tall covenantal fence all the way around it. But because the one flesh union occurs any time there is a sexual union, whether moral or immoral, we must sanctify and seal the sexual union with a covenantal oath. When a sexual union is sealed with a lawful covenantal oath, it is called marriage.

When a new family is formed, it is formed around a sexual relationship. The Bible teaches us that this marriage relationship portrays Christ and the church. Just as the husband and wife are physically united as one, so Christ and the church are spiritually one. When a husband and wife have a physical union along with spiritual harmony, then it provides a good picture of Christ and the church. A couple who have this physical union, but who are constantly fighting, are *constantly lying* about Christ and the church.

A husband and wife do not have the option of saying nothing about Christ and the church. If the husband and wife are driving down the street, and some woman who is almost wearing a dress walks by, and he almost drives off the road, then the whole world knows that his wife has been insulted. But the world does not really know *why*. The husband is saying that, even though Jesus singled out a people for Himself, and then shed His blood for His elect, He is still willing to gawk at strangers. The lie says that Christ is unfaithful to His elect. So mental or physical infidelity is telling a lie about the spiritual faithfulness of Jesus to His people. Christian couples must protect their sexual and spiritual harmony, keeping that unity free from all disruptions. Otherwise, we lie to the world about Christ and the church.

When the lie is present, the children in the home usually have the front row seats. If the children of this sexual union are to have a high view of the Christian church, then they must be shown and taught to have a high view of their mother. If their mother is loved and treated by their father the way Christ loves the church, then their father is telling them the truth about Jesus and the church. This testimony includes a visible sexual devotion.

The Bible tells us clearly that we are to have nothing to do with sexual immorality. We are even to avoid *verbal* jesting about immorality. "But fornication and all uncleanness or covetousness, let it not even be named among you, as is fitting the saints; neither filthiness, nor foolish talking, nor coarse jesting, which are not fitting, but rather giving of thanks" (Eph. 5:3–4).

But some have taken the biblical instruction at this point to mean that there should never be mention of sexual morality either. But the Bible says that in the Christian community there must not be a hint of sexual *immorality*. We should be pure in our conversations and in our entertainment. It does not say ". . . but among you there must not be a hint of sex." The sexual relationship between the husband and the wife is not sexual immorality. There is nothing wrong with children knowing that their father is male and their mother is female and that they have a sexual relationship. There is something wrong with them *not* knowing this. Tragically, there are many children who can easily imagine their parents sitting in front of the television set laughing at dirty jokes, while they cannot comprehend that their mother and father have a sexual relationship. They cannot comprehend their parents involved in *moral* sexual behavior, but they can see them involved in immorality. This is a profound tragedy.

That there is a sexual relationship at the center of the home should be obvious to all who live there—hugs, kisses, and romantic attention. If the children know that there is a fundamental unity between husband and wife, they can easily understand the spiritual analogy of Christ and His people. "This is a great mystery, but I speak concerning Christ and the church" (Eph. 5:32).

Christians often have a view of sexual relations that is out of balance because they have allowed themselves to be propagandized through the world's entertainment industry. But suppose one afternoon a neighbor came to a Christian's door and said something like this.

"We would like to invite you over this evening . . ."

"Why, thank you!" he says, innocently enough.

"Wait, wait, that's not all. We would like to invite you to come into our bedroom and watch us while we have sex. It could be a really exciting time for all of us."

The Christian recoils in horror. "We couldn't do that. You see, we're Christians."

"Oh, I see," he says, scratching his head. "That could be a little much for you then. I'll tell you what! We have a video camera. Why don't you let us tape it, and I'll just bring it over in the morning. Then you watch it whenever you want."

The Christian explains that this wouldn't be possible either.

"I don't understand," the neighbor says, with a puzzled look. "Last week you invited us over and we all watched that movie on your VCR. It had a couple of skin scenes in it. Why are you willing to watch another's man wife, but not mine? My wife may not be the best looking . . ."

Here the hapless Christian interrupts and explains that her looks have nothing to do with it. He goes on to explain that they are not ordinary Christians. They belong to that very special breed—*hypocrites*.

Is hypocrisy too strong a word? I don't believe so. Many Christians are willing to watch, by means of a movie camera, what they wouldn't dream of watching in person. You couldn't get them into a topless bar, and yet they cheerfully go to films where they see far more. Would most Christian men be willing to be peeping Toms, roving the neighborhood? Certainly not. But what if they discovered a woman who knew of their presence and was willing to undress in front of the window? That would be worse. What if she were paid to do all this? Worse, worse, and still worse. And if she is paid lots of money, has a producer and director, does all this for the movie cameras, and has *millions* of men drooling at her window sill? This is suddenly different and becomes quite a "complicated" issue.

Some try to excuse this sort of behavior on the basis of contemporary standards. Christians don't want to be different in what they watch. They don't want to admit that their discipleship applies to this area. And they also don't want to admit that sexual activity and nudity on the screen is sexually exciting for them.

But those who deny that such things affect them are simply deceiving themselves. There is no way to watch— for *entertainment*—bed scenes or displays of nudity without being affected negatively in some way. But there *are* men who deny that such things affect them. Such denials come from two kinds of men. The first group are liars. They are either lying to themselves or to the listener and most probably to both. The man is excited or aroused by what he sees, but as a Christian, he knows it is not socially acceptable to say so. So he comes out of the theater with his Christian friends, speaking this way: "That was a really good movie. Shame about that one scene, though." But in his heart, that one scene was the morsel he kept under his tongue.

There is another man who denies that it affects him, and he is telling the truth. But why is he not aroused? Because his heart is hard, and his conscience has been seared. "To the pure all things are pure, but to those who are de-

filed and unbelieving nothing is pure; but even their mind
and conscience are defiled" (Titus 1:15). He is so dead-
ened in his conscience that it would take a lot more than
that to get him going.

But the heart can be very deceitful. There is a third
way to sin in this sort of thing. This response recognizes
the impact that such material has, and attempts to use it.
People, even Christians, frequently justify viewing or reading
immoral material by saying that it helps them in their sex
lives at home. "It doesn't matter where you get your appetite, as long as you eat at home." This approach at least
has the virtue of honesty. It admits that sexually explicit
material is sexually exciting. But it is terribly flawed.

The first response is to point out that the Bible expressly
tells men where their satisfaction and excitement should
be. It should be in their wives alone. I was once talking to
a Christian man about the sort of films he watched. He justified himself in this way: "When I see another woman's
body in a film, I imagine my wife's face on her." The Bible
clearly contradicts this kind of thinking: ". . . and rejoice
with the wife of your youth . . . let her breasts satisfy you
at all times; and always be enraptured with her love"
(Prov.5:18–19). This means that a man should see to it that
his wife *alone* is the basis of his sexual excitement and satisfaction. Other women, whether in films, books, or magazines, must not be the source of his arousal. As soon as
other women get into a husband's sexual thinking, then
Christ's clear prohibition applies: "But I say to you that
whoever looks at a woman to lust for her has already committed adultery with her in his heart" (Matt. 5:28).

The second response is flatly to deny that this kind of
thing helps couples in their sex lives. The introduction of
others into a sexual relationship (whether the others are
two-dimensional or not) can only be a source of long-term
frustration. This is because it inevitably introduces comparisons, and such comparisons are destructive in a godly
covenantal relationship.

This is not to deny the *short-term* excitement that such things introduce. If it were not exciting, then people wouldn't do it. But short-term excitement and intensity do not justify a practice. Ten women can give a man a better time in bed than one woman can—for a short while. But this is simply purchasing short-term intense pleasure with long-term grief. These women cannot provide helpful companionship or bring up his children better than one woman can.

A couple can gain short-term excitement from movies, books, or magazines that range from suggestive to explicit. But that does not make it right. Lust always demands more excitement—always more, more! Consequently, lust attempts to get from a finite thing what only the infinite can provide. The trade-off for this excitement is long-term frustration and dissatisfaction. The wife cannot be as exciting as some of these performing cows of Bashan, and the husband does not have the sexual stamina or prowess that such materials imply he should have. So both the man and the woman have agreed *to compare themselves to a lie.* Sex in the real world is not at all like what they have come to accept from the world of sexual fiction. But because they have agreed with the lie that whatever a couple has is "not enough," they will always be dissatisfied with what God has given them.

The foundation is this: in order to be under the blessing of God we must *accept our creaturely limitations.* If they are accepted wisely, the limitations themselves are recognized as a blessing.

What are some of these limitations? A man is limited to one woman. A man is limited to a finite amount of sexual pleasure. He is limited, and all such limitations are a great blessing from God. In short, it is good to be a creature. The way we think has long-term consequences; this, *and only this*, is a defense of lasting sexual pleasure.

Men in rebellion against God have trouble understanding the importance of the distinction between the Creator and the creature. This is because all rebellion against God is rooted, ultimately, in a desire to *replace* Him. Men do not just want to flee from the authority of God; they want to topple Him. This may not mean there is always a conscious desire to overthrow the Creator. Nor does it mean that God is worried about the possibility of their success. But it certainly means that, whether conscious or not, these unsuccessful attempts to "become as God" will result in chaos in the lives of the rebels. And when the rebellion is sexual in nature, the chaos is sexual in nature.

The central problem with such lust is the steadfast refusal to tolerate limits. As mentioned above, lust is the desire to receive from a finite thing what only the infinite can provide. It seeks to elevate the created (sexual activity) to the level of God. But because we are finite, our sexual pleasures are also finite. This means that there has to be an end to it. But lust is incapable of saying "enough." There must always be something else, something more. There is pleasure—but never satisfaction. It is for this reason that lust will always lead to various perversions. Once all the possible pleasure has been squeezed out of the finite sexual limits given to us by God, lust demands new territory. The fact that the new territory is hostile to true sexual pleasure does not deter the person controlled by his lust. He charges ahead, little knowing that he is destroying the thing he worships.

We must return again to 1 Thessalonians 4:3–5—"For this is the will of God, your sanctification: that you should abstain from sexual immorality; that each of you should know how to possess his own vessel in sanctification and honor, not in passion of lust, like the Gentiles who do not know God . . ." It is important to notice how Paul connects sexual morality with a knowledge of God. If the infinite triune God of the Bible is denied, then at some point (at least in the minds of rebellious men), something must be sought to replace Him.

For those in the grip of lust, the created thing they idolize is sexuality. And the fate of this created thing is the same as all other created things promoted to "Deity." Incapable of becoming God, it only becomes a twisted creature, which is then worshipped and served by its devotees—other twisted and bent creatures. But this idol, like all idols, will then topple and fall. It will have eyes that cannot see, ears that cannot hear, and hands that cannot love.

The Bible tells us to be renewed in our *minds*. We must learn to think differently about the way we live, and we must never forget that our sexual nature and our lovemaking constitute a sizeable portion of our lives. Because of this, Christians should avoid *any* compromise with the world at this point. We must not compromise with the world when it is wanton, or when it is reactionary and prudish. In other words, we should be different—or as the Bible puts it, *holy*. This means Christians must pursue sexual holiness.

The Discipline of Faithfulness

God created us male and female. So much is obvious; but the way He did it was instructive. When the Lord Jesus taught on the subject of divorce, He appealed to the creation ordinance of marriage found in the early chapters of Genesis. He taught us that *God* puts a man and woman together in marriage, and what God has joined together man has no authority to separate. The temptation is to argue that in Genesis God only joined together Adam and Eve—two individuals. But this argument resists the teaching of Christ, who insisted that Adam and Eve were a paradigmatic couple. When God joined *them* together, He was joining together *every* man and woman who has ever come together sexually in a covenant bond.

Other facts are obvious as well from this creation ordinance of marriage. Because God created Adam and Eve, homosexuality is excluded. Because Adam could find no helper for himself among the animals, bestiality is excluded. And because God created just *one* woman for Adam, the pattern of monogamy was set and displayed to us.

The case for monogamy would therefore be an easy one if it were not for the polygamy found in the Old Testament among the saints of God. How are we to understand this? First, we see polygamy was instituted by *man*, and not by God. The first record of a polygamous union was Lamech (Gen. 4:19), with no hint of divine approval. But still, even recognizing the human origin of polygamy, we see that many of God's saints in the Old Testament had more than one woman at one time—Abraham, Jacob, David, *et al.*

In addressing the question, we must first recognize it is not merely academic. This is not vaporizing over a bunch of nothing. We are living in a culture which is conducting a full-scale assault on the biblical definition of the family. If there is no biblical reformation of our culture, then polygamous unions will soon be legal in the United States. When this happens, what will the attitude of the church be? And *why*? We cannot respond with Victorian platitudes; our response must be thoroughly biblical. We must build a theology of marriage which takes *all* of Scripture into account, including the polygamy of the Old Testament saints.

The first point of response is to remember the creation ordinance. God created us to live *as couples*. As Christians our desire should be to live out that design.

Second, in the New Testament, we are taught that every married couple is a representation of Christ and the church. Sinful rebellious couples are not just destroying their own lives, they are lying about Christ. Christ is the Bridegroom, and the Church is His Bride. Because Christ has only one Bride, a polygamous marriage is a flawed and distorted representation of Him. Polygamy is therefore to be avoided by all consistent Christians; it is dishonoring to the Lord of faithfulness.

This understanding of marriage explains why an elder in a Christian church is *required* to be a "one woman man" (1 Tim. 3:2; Titus 1:6). The elders are to set a pattern and example for the rest of the saints (Heb. 13:7, 17). Consequently, the Bible absolutely forbids polygamy in the leadership of the church. At the same time, in a culture where polygamy is legal, a polygamist may be admitted to *membership* in the church. For example, if a man with three wives in a primitive tribe is converted, what must he do? Unlike an adulterer or homosexual, a polygamist cannot walk away from this sin. He should remain married to his wives. A man can only flee polygamy through divorce, which is *another* sin. Such a man must not be allowed leadership in the church because this is not the pattern for Christian marriage. Nonetheless, the Old Testament examples show us that polygamy can be tolerated in a limited way.

As we prepare for such a time, Christian men must learn to discipline themselves in their faithfulness to their own wives. "For this is the will of God, your sanctification: that you should abstain from sexual immorality; that each of you should know how to possess his own vessel in sanctification and honor, not in passion of lust, like the Gentiles who do not know God . . ." (1 Thess. 4:3–5). There are two clear aspects of this.

The first is resistance to infidelity, or as Paul puts it, abstention from immorality. Christ was blunt about the subject of lust, and we live in a culture which does not really encourage the women to wear lots of clothes. We are all surrounded by visual harlotry of all kinds—in magazines, movies, books. There are manifold daily enticements to infidelity. The word of God to Christian men is clear—*abstain*.

The second aspect of Paul's instruction requires devoted attention to wives. In this passage, the attention shown is certainly sexual. The sexual possession of a man's vessel is to be accomplished in "sanctification and honor." The author of Hebrews says the same—"Marriage is honorable among all, and the bed undefiled; but fornicators and adulterers God will judge" (Heb. 13:4).

There are dangers *outside* the mind as well. Often husbands fail to build a sufficiently high fence around the covenant relationship of marriage. They do this by allowing *one-on-one* relationships to develop with members of the opposite sex outside the immediate family. A man may allow a relationship with a female friend to grow—and she is not his wife, mother, sister, daughter, or grandmother. A wife may be close to a man not her husband, father, brother, son, or grandfather. This is foolhardy; when two individuals are on guard against physical intimacy only, they are allowing other forms of intimacy to grow unwatched. To guard against this, a married couple should befriend others, and function socially, *as a couple.*

Christian men ought not refrain from the sexual pollutions that surround us because they object to lovemaking; they refrain because they object to the wanton *vandalism* of it. Our culture is doing to sex what people who chew with their mouths open do to food. The Bible teaches us that lovemaking is to be *honored* among Christians; to honor something means to *esteem it highly*. Those Christians who have reacted to public immorality by retreating into a blue-nosed prudishness in their *own* bedrooms are very much a part of the problem.

CHAPTER EIGHT

Multiplying Fruitfully

The Blessing of Children

If one were to get out a concordance to look up the issue of birth control, he will be quickly disappointed. There is nothing in Scripture that bears explicitly on the subject. But this does not mean that Scripture is silent here. Birth control is, after all, an activity which seeks to regulate the number of *children*, and on *that* subject the Bible has a great deal to say.

As many Christians have come to recognize, our culture has a lousy attitude towards kids. Because this bad attitude is so apparent, some Christians have reacted to this sin and have come to maintain that large families are an unqualified blessing, no matter what. This is obviously much closer to the truth than the anti-child mindset, but something is still missing.

Large families can be a great blessing. So as the Bible makes clear, when we hear about a family with seven children, we have no grounds for rolling our eyes heavenward, and making snide comments. "Don't they know what *causes* this?" Tragically, such comments are frequently heard, even at church, and from Christians who have been thoroughly compromised by the world's hostile attitude towards children. *They* are going to have their allotted 1.7 children, pop the kids into daycare six weeks after birth, and pursue their dual careers. But the Scripture presents a view of children which is entirely antithetical to this. "Behold, children are a heritage from the Lord, the fruit of the womb is a reward. Like arrows in the hand of a warrior, so are the children of one's youth. Happy is the man who has his quiver full of them; they shall not be ashamed, but shall speak with their enemies in the gate" (Ps. 127:3–5).

So it is good that more and more Christians are coming to see just how horrible it is for the Christian church to have a bigoted attitude toward little ones. But there is another aspect to the issue that reactionary Christians do not see as well. The Bible also teaches that children are a blessing—*or a curse*. It follows that a large number of children are a large blessing—*or a large curse*. "A foolish son is a grief to his father, and bitterness to her who bore him" (Prov. 17:25). When children are brought up in the Lord, and they walk with Him when they are grown, the blessing this brings to parents is unspeakable. And the more this happens, *the better it is.* Large, *obedient* families are a blessing. But when the children are disobedient, the more there are, the worse it is. Samuel would not have been more greatly blessed if he had had five sons who took bribes instead of two (1 Sam. 8:3). Joel and Abijah were enough.

The passage from Psalm 127 noted above is frequently cited by Christians as they talk about the blessings of family. This is good, but we must notice what the real blessing is. The psalm is not talking about the patter of little feet around the house (although, of course, that is nice). The psalm says that sons are like arrows to a man when he contends with his enemies in the gate. The blessing being referred to here is the blessing of *grown* sons, well brought up, and prepared for battle. This is the result of a man spending himself for several decades on his children. If a man has a large number of sons, and he has not reared them properly, he has a quiver full all right, but it is a quiver full of grief—crooked and broken arrows.

What does it take to have a large number of children? All that is necessary is a physically mature male and female. What does it take to have a large blessing? Receiving the blessing the Bible associates with large families requires a great deal more than the simple biological capacity for reproduction. A commitment to the blessing of a large family means that a man must also be committed to love, hard work, thoughtfulness, self-sacrifice, tenderness, and discipline over a period of many years.

Some husbands think they have a commitment to the biblical view of family just because they are male, opinionated, and dislike condoms. These are the men who are headed for grief (in the form of fools for sons) and who are leading their wives into bitterness. Our Lord spoke of the folly of a man who undertook the building of a tower without the resources to complete the task. How much greater is the folly when the task undertaken is one that involves one's own family. Presumption in the conception of large numbers of children is no virtue. Unless the Lord builds the house, the one who labors builds in vain (Ps. 127:1).

Of course, this is not promotion of birth control. It simply recognizes that any biblical doctrine or teaching will always face a double threat. The first, of course, is the threat posed by those who resist and oppose the teaching directly. Sadly, many professing Christians resist the blessings of the family. But we must guard ourselves against the common failure of fighting off the *other* fellow's temptations. If we accept the biblical teaching on the blessing of children, we must ask ourselves what *our* temptations will be.

This questioning is necessary because the second threat to any teaching is posed by those who profess to embrace it, and who then proceed to shipwreck it. No greater instrument of slander is given to those who resist the truth than when adherents of the "truth" do what any fool, saint, scoundrel, wise man, or high school sophomore can do (*i.e.*, beget a child), and who then fail to bring that child up in the fear of the Lord. The former is easy and involves a good deal of pleasure. The latter is hard and involves a good deal of pain, Christ-like sacrifice and love—husbandry.

The Lord said that when someone stumbles a little one it would be better for him that a millstone be tied around his neck and he be thrown into the sea. What then are we to make of a male who begets little ones he will not teach, fathers children he will not feed, and sires offspring he will not pastor? As if one millstone were not enough, he has demanded more. The Lord is just and will grant his request.

When we first appreciate the severity of this situation, our natural temptation is to run off with our talent and bury it in the ground. Our Lord can appear at first glance to be a "hard master." We are tempted to respond to the Bible's teaching on family the same way Christ's disciples responded to His teaching on marriage—"It is better not to be married!" We say (or perhaps think), "If this is the way it is, it is better not to have children!" But irresponsibility provides no refuge at all—it does not matter if the irresponsibility is seen through no children or through seven children left without a shepherd.

So this is not written to scare young couples away from the blessings of family. Rather, it is written to show that the blessing is not easy or automatic. The Lord offers to bless us with much in our children, and to whom much is given, much is required.

The Long Run

> "Her children rise up and call her blessed; her husband also, and he praises her: 'Many daughters have done well, but you excel them all' (Prov. 31: 28–29).

More and more young couples are deciding to trust God in the area of family planning—ready to receive as many "as God sends." At the time the decision is made they both feel very good about it. But after they have been married for five years, the young husband finds himself with four pre-school children and one wife with second thoughts.

How can a husband in such a situation encourage his wife? The first thing he should do is seek to determine what some of the possible sources of discouragement are. In what follows, I supply a few suggestions for encouragement geared to some of the temptations encountered by Christian women who are bearing children.

A principal cause of discouragement is exhaustion. If a mother is doing her job at home with her little ones, she will be far more physically tired than she used to be before they arrived. What can the husband do?

First, he can help in two ways: by helping with the kids and also through refraining from acting like an extra kid himself. He should also help by watching the troops so that his wife can get out by herself at least once a week. He should also arrange for a regular babysitter so that *he* can take her out—she needs a sabbath.

Second, he should recognize that the kids are placing demands on his wife's body all day long—they want to nurse, they want to be carried, they want to be held, etc. This means that he should be sensitive to how he approaches her sexually. He must not be just one more voice in the clamor.

Third, he must teach his wife to look for the long-term blessing, both in this life and the next. The most important returns from child-rearing in this life do not come in the first five years. When the children are little, we have to invest more time and energy. But if they are disciplined and taught well, as they grow they will begin to contribute far more to the family than they receive from it. We are born into this world with one mouth and two hands. So when we are obedient to God, we produce more than we consume. But initially, as newborns and toddlers, children merely contribute to the workload.

So a husband should encourage his wife by reminding her of the eternal value of the work she is doing. When she and her children have been there ten thousand years, bright shining as the sun, then that *apparently* eternal pile of laundry will finally come into perspective.

Child-bearing can also be discouraging because of the hostility of the world and "well-meaning" Christians. One time my wife and just two (!) of our children were stopped on the street by an older women who said, "My! You don't believe in the pill, do you?" The mental picture that unbelievers have of a fruitful woman is one who looks like she was dragged through a knothole, with a small regiment of runny-nosed idiots hanging onto the hem of her tattered dress. In the face of such hostility, the encouragement the husband must supply is obvious. He must not only appreciate the work she is doing for him, he must let her know constantly how much he appreciates it.

Related to this is the importance of honoring pregnancy. Throughout Scripture, we see fruitfulness exalted. One of the most valuable things I ever learned from my father was the loveliness of a pregnant woman. So instead of mockery and flippant jokes, Christians should honor those whom the Lord has blessed. And it is also important that a Christian husband honor his wife in tangible ways. One such thing he should do is aimed directly at his wife's temptation of "feeling dowdy." The Bible teaches that one of the central responsibilities of a husband is to keep his wife in clothes (Ex. 21:10). The wife need not be clothed ostentatiously (indeed, such is prohibited), but a husband should see to it that his wife is able to dress nicely all the time, but particularly during pregnancy.

Another source of discouragement is found in the temptation of assuming too much about the providence of God over the future. We have all been taught by the anti-children crowd that if a couple with a normal sexual appetite refrains from using birth control, the necessary and inexorable result will always be approximately forty-two children before menopause. But as the fellow said, "It ain't necessarily so." And when there are more than just a few children, God remains faithful—He never betrays our trust. For example, the Lord blessed us with three children within the first five years of our marriage. Under such circumstances, it is very easy for a wife to start doing story problems in her head. (A woman has one child every 18–24 months for 4 years. She has twenty years of fertility left. What is wrong with that woman?) The problem with such thinking is that it is based on a false and unbiblical premise—*i.e.,* that the universe is an impersonal place and that the providence of God has little or nothing to do with the blessings we receive. In our case, although we would have welcomed more children, the Lord has not added to our family over the last fourteen years.

Some couples who do not use birth control have ten children, some have three, and some have not been blessed with any. The Bible teaches that the number is not the result of chance; the Lord is the One who opens and closes wombs. I am not arguing here that birth control is unlawful. But Christians who use birth control must not do so because they accept the lies of pagans who have a low view of children.

So to keep his wife encouraged, a husband's top priority should be her spiritual and emotional contentment. She should be in his prayers, and she should know that she is. She should be frequently held, comforted, counseled, and taught by her husband from the Word of God. While some in the world may despise her calling and vocation, she should be praised in it often by a grateful husband. It is truly a high calling. "Nevertheless she will be saved in childbearing if they continue in faith, love, and holiness, with self-control"(1 Tim. 2:15). Instead of a bedraggled appearance and a large number of children demonstrating to the cynic how often she makes love, her beautiful appearance and well kempt children should demonstrate how much she *is* loved.

So What About Birth Control?

In one sense, the fact that birth control is an issue in the church again is a good sign. No longer are Christians automatically assuming that a practice which is widespread in the world must be legitimate. At the same time, just because multitudes of non-Christians are doing something does not automatically make it unlawful either. So how are we to approach the question?

The first step is to see if the Bible teaches directly on the subject. And at this level it is clear that *certain forms* of birth control are expressly prohibited in Scripture. Beginning with the most obvious, we may exclude infanticide and abortion. The Bible excludes all such practices in the most direct way possible—"Thou shalt not kill." What many may not realize is that this commandment also excludes certain birth control devices, such as "morning after pills" or the IUD. These are devices which prevent the implantation of a fertilized egg. Consequently, they are unlawfully taking a human life after it has begun.

But what about other birth control devices? Does the Bible say anything about the lawfulness of a husband and wife limiting the number of children they have or spacing them? The answer is both yes and no. There is nothing in Scripture that says the act of using birth control is unlawful in itself. At the same time, most birth control as practiced today is sinful in its motivation and application. To understand this we have to look at a related subject first.

While the Bible says nothing about birth control, as stated earlier, it teaches much about children and family. So before we can ask whether the practice of birth control is lawful, we have to ask whether or not it springs from an understanding of, and submission to, the Bible's teaching on the family. And because situations vary, sometimes it does and much of the time it does not.

Let us start with an example of a situation where the use of birth control would not be godly. Suppose a couple is thinking this way: "You know, kids are a hassle, both our careers are going well right now, the world is really over-populated, and besides, we can always go off the pill later." Nothing is more apparent than the fact that this couple has been drinking in worldly assumptions from a fire hose.

Now a counter-example: "The Lord has graciously given us six children, and they are all a delight to us. But we have recently been thinking about using birth control because it is getting harder and harder to provide them with the care the Bible requires. We are starting to have trouble feeding them all—and the tuition costs for a biblical education (or the time costs for a biblical home education) really add up."

Now the second couple may be mistaken in their assumptions (about their ability to care for seven children, for example). But this mistaken assumption is not the same kind of thing as the sinful and rebellious attitude exhibited by the first couple. In contrast, we see a family which believes that children are a blessing, and they have been acting accordingly.

Because the Bible says nothing about birth control itself, we must evaluate the action based upon whether the action is motivated by a biblical attitude toward that which the Bible does address—children and family.

Some have argued that the case of Onan spilling his seed on the ground in Genesis is an example of God's judgment on an act of birth control. And so it was—but here our point (about the primacy of motivation) is strengthened. The thing that was objectionable in Onan's action was his deliberate attempt to rob his deceased brother of his posterity (Gen. 38:9). In other words, judgment fell on him because his motives were evil. Consequently, those who practice birth control with ungodly motives are following in the footsteps of Onan. But it takes a good deal of ingenuity to make a connection between this evil motive of Onan's and the motive of a godly couple who practice birth control to space their children in order to *maximize* the number of children they can have (e.g., because she has to deliver by

Caesarean section). So when there is no clear teaching in
the Scripture on a subject of moral and ethical behavior, it
is necessary for us to be silent. We may not condemn something as sin in itself simply on the grounds that most people
who do it are sinful in their motivations.

But this does not mean that a Christian husband and
wife practicing birth control are free to assume they are
doing right. It is true, as argued above, that this entire issue must be understood in the light of our motivations, and
our submission to the scriptural view of family. It is also
true that in the area of motivations, we are answerable to
God and Him alone. The issue of birth control is not an
area where the civil magistrate or the elders of the church
have any business. If an ungodly attitude toward children
and family is visible and apparent, then *that* should be addressed by the elders of a church. But they should deal
with it the same way they would deal with an analogous
situation (e.g., someone who has an ungodly attitude toward alcohol—a substance not sinful in itself but which can
be abused).

Parents are stewards before God, and God entrusts the
children to them. Some parents receive the resources which
God gives and bring up many children to serve Him. They
are greatly blessed. Other parents may limit the children
they have but believe the children they have to be a great
blessing, and they also bring them up to serve the Lord.
These parents are also blessed by God. When Jesus told
the parable of the talents, He did not refer to any quarrel
between the man who had ten talents and the man who had
five. The one who got into trouble (with his master, and
not with his fellow-servants) was the one who feared to
be entrusted with any responsibility. He buried what he
had in the ground and was condemned by his master. And
this is what many Christian couples have done and are doing. They don't want the responsibility of parenthood, but
God has said that He made them one for the purpose of
godly offspring (Mal. 2:15).

So our modern debate about birth control has unfortunately gravitated to the methods used—as if the lazy servant could have justified himself by pointing out that the action of burying money in the ground is not inherently sinful. This is true enough, but beside the point.

Nowhere in the Bible does it say that the use of birth control is sinful. So it is wrong to say that it is. The Bible does consistently say that children are a blessing from the Lord. And it is a sin to say or act as though they are not.

CHAPTER NINE

Divorce and Remarriage

Divorce

Divorce is the dissolution of a marriage. As we have seen, a marriage exists when there has been a sexual union within the context of a covenantal oath (Mal. 2:14). When that covenant is violated, then the marriage itself has been violated.

A marriage does not exist simply because a couple has become one flesh. Paul uses the term *one flesh* in describing a man's relationship with a prostitute (1 Cor. 6:16), which is obviously not a marriage. A marriage exists when a heterosexual sexual relationship has been *sanctified with an oath*. So then, marriage requires that a couple become one flesh, but it also requires a covenantal oath.

This helps us understand why God hates divorce. "For the Lord God of Israel says that He hates divorce . . ." (Mal. 2:16a). God hates divorce because a central purpose of the marriage covenant is to produce godly offspring (Mal. 2:15). Divorce squanders the opportunity that parents have to train up godly children before the Lord. In addition, because divorce is a violation of the marriage covenant, God hates the falsehood involved. He is a covenant-keeping God, and He hates the slander of covenants which faithlessness in marriages involves.

Because God hates divorce, it is not surprising that some have concluded that divorce is *always* a sin. Unfortunately, this position does not do justice to all the biblical teaching on the subject. Of course, it is *always* sin for at least one of the marriage partners. It is usually sin for both. Nevertheless, it is sometimes an act of righteousness for the offended and innocent party.

This does not mean that divorce is automatically legitimate for the innocent party. It can be legitimate, but it frequently is not. There is a difference between being "in the right" and being *right*. The innocent party may be innocent with regard to the final point under dispute. But this does not mean that he or she is innocent in the behavior leading up to that point. Nor does it mean that the "innocent party" will conduct himself without bitterness or rancor during the dispute. So someone might have the right, or even obligation, to divorce his or her partner, but still do it in the wrong way.

For a concrete example, suppose a Christian woman has been married for ten years. Her husband (not a Christian) has been a practicing homosexual for the last five years. She has just found out about it, and he is completely unrepentant. Does she have the right to divorce him? Yes, and she probably *ought* to. And if she does so, then she has also the right to remarry.

But this does not mean she is immune to temptation and sin in pursuing the divorce. Whether she sins or not depends on how she conducts herself. Is she doing it because she is concerned to do the righteous thing before the Lord? Or is she bitter, malicious and spiteful? The temptation will always be to say, "But look what he did to *me!*" But even in such difficult circumstances, she must also look at the attitude Jesus commanded his followers to have when they are mistreated. True forgiveness can only be extended when a *real wrong* has been done. And his behavior qualifies—it is really wrong.

Many times a woman in such a situation refuses to forgive because she assumes that if she forgives him she will have to stay with him. But this does not necessarily follow. That would depend on whether he has given up the homosexual behavior, whether he has AIDS, whether he has become a Christian, *etc.* And even then it is up to her to decide—so long as she is acting biblically and not seeking to justify her bitterness with a prooftext.

At the same time, she should examine her own behavior over the ten years of their marriage. Did she seek to win him to the Lord the way the Bible instructs (1 Pet. 3:1–6), or did she live with him in her own way, and on her own terms? If the latter, then she must acknowledge that sin to God *before* she decides to pursue a divorce. Otherwise, she does not have a clear understanding of the failure of the marriage and of the years prior to his violation of the covenant.

Some will perhaps object that this is making her feel guilty for the breakup of the marriage, when the husband was the responsible individual. But of course it is his responsibility. The husband is the head of the household. This means that he is the steward of the covenant, even if he is not a Christian and has no concept of the covenant. Nevertheless, she must still understand, as an individual Christian, where she did not obey God. This in no way lessens the gravity of his sin. It merely enables her to decide what she should do with the clear vision that forgiveness supplies.

Now because the husband is the steward of the marriage covenant, the gender of the innocent party does matter in making decisions about divorce. The Christian community is full of godly Christian women who have non-Christian husbands. Godly Christian men with non-Christian wives are much more rare. This illustrates how much of an impact the husband has on the spiritual state of the marriage.

In relating this to divorce, it means that wives are much more likely to be wronged by their husbands than the other way around. If a man is unfaithful to his wife, it is quite possible that she was being the kind of wife God wants her to be. If a woman is unfaithful to her husband, it is much less likely that he was fulfilling his role properly.

This does not mean that he cannot divorce her, but it

does mean that he must assume *full* responsibility for what
he has done (or, more likely, *not* done). If he assumes this
responsibility, he is in a much better position to do what
God wants him to do. In other words, if the innocent party
is the husband, it is very likely that the innocence has some
significant blemishes.

This is not a universal law, but it is a general pattern.
Some exceptions would obviously include situations where
the marriage had deteriorated before he became a Christian. In such a situation, the marriage might be too far gone
to save, or the wife may want nothing to do with Christ.
The one thing to remember, as a general rule, is that the
innocent party (man or woman) has access to many resources
in the form of biblical teaching. These resources are rarely
used.

It is uncommon to see a situation where the innocent
party goes into a divorce with a godly attitude. I have seen
a number of situations where there were biblical grounds
for divorce. But I have not seen many where the situation
was handled with a biblical attitude. By God's grace, that
has sometimes been turned around. And usually, when the
attitude is corrected, the possibility of a godly reconciliation is much greater.

Biblical Grounds for Divorce

Before addressing the grounds for divorce, we should recognize the distinction made between those who understand
God's law from the outside and those who understand it
from within. Those who understand the law from the outside will simply use it as a checklist. "Ah, here it is. I get
to divorce him." But those who understand the *covenantal nature of marriage* will see why God sets down the requirements He does. They will also be prepared for any
possible reconciliation.

Nevertheless there are three basic categories. In the
nature of the case, there is, of course, some overlap.

First, in Matthew 5:31–32, Jesus says this: "Furthermore it has been said, 'Whoever divorces his wife, let him give her a certificate of divorce.' But I say to you that whoever divorces his wife for any reason except sexual immorality causes her to commit adultery; and whoever marries a woman who is divorced commits adultery."

The word translated here as "sexual immorality" is *porneias*. It means sexual uncleanness or fornication. It is not the specific word for adultery used later in this passage, although adultery would certainly be included as a type of *porneias*. Such behavior includes immorality *before* marriage that the other person did not know about. "Then Joseph her husband, being *a just man*, and not wanting to make her a public example, was minded to put her away secretly" (Matt. 1:19). Although Joseph was mistaken about the facts of the case, and although the marriage was not yet consummated, the passage is still instructive. If a man thought he was marrying a virgin, and three months into the marriage she turned up six months pregnant by another man, the *porneias* clause would apply.

Porneias is a general term. It applies to sexual immorality before and after marriage. In the Greek Old Testament, the word is closely linked with idolatry. Given the nature of pagan idolatry, the linkage is probably not entirely figurative, because the idolatry frequently involved immorality during worship.

Because marriage is a covenant surrounding the sexual relationship, sexual immorality strikes at the heart of that covenant. In such a case, the innocent party may, without sin, divorce his spouse. But if there is any opportunity for a *godly* reconciliation, it should certainly be encouraged.

The second biblical ground for divorce is addressed in 1 Corinthians 7:12–16. Paul says:

> But to the rest I, not the Lord, say: If any brother has a wife who does not believe, and she is willing to live with him, let him not divorce her. And a woman who has a

husband who does not believe, if he is willing to live with
her, let her not divorce him. For the unbelieving husband
is sanctified by the wife, and the unbelieving wife is sanctified by the husband; otherwise your children would be
unclean, but now they are holy. But if the unbeliever de-
parts, let him depart; a brother or a sister is *not under
bondage in such cases*. But God has called us to peace. For
how do you know, O wife, whether you will save your
husband? Or how do you know, O husband, whether
you will save your wife?

The issue in this passage is *covenantal desertion*. If the
non-Christian is willing to live within the Christian understanding of the marriage covenant (as well as a non-Christian can; that is to say, externally), then he is sanctified.
*This means that he receives an external blessing as a result of
external conformity to God's standard*. It does *not* mean that
he can be saved without placing his faith in Christ. But if
he decides to desert his spouse, the Christian is *not bound*.
What is more, the Christian is forbidden to fight the divorce. This means that the Christian is free—free to remarry, free to stay single, and free to reconcile with his
partner (as long as there has not been another marriage in
between [Deut. 24:1–4]). Not bound means *not bound*.

The third class involves the violation of biblical laws
that carried the death penalty. For example, in a just society, a mass murderer would be put to death. In ours, this
frequently does not happen. Where does this leave the
murderer's spouse?

If the civil government were doing its God-appointed
task (*i.e.*, punishing the wrongdoer with the sword
[Rom. 13:4]), then divorce would have occurred *by means
of execution*. But if the civil government fails to do its appointed task, then the two remaining governments (family and church) have a choice to make.

The fact that godly executions do not occur should not
deter those governments that do not have the power of the
sword. The church should excommunicate, and a godly

spouse may divorce. Both actions are *not* a removal of the offending party from the appropriate covenant. They are a legal recognition that the person has already removed himself.

This is not mere theory. The Bible gives us an example of families and the church taking action in just this way. In Ezra 9:1, it states, "When these things were done, the leaders came to me, saying, 'The people of Israel and the priests and the Levites have not separated themselves from the peoples of the lands, *with respect to the abominations* of the Canaanites, the Hittites, the Perizzites, the Jebusites, the Ammonites, the Moabites, the Egyptians, and the Amorites.'

Ezra was appalled, and in the next chapter he requires the Israelite men who had sinned in this way to put away their foreign wives. It is important to note that the issue was not the *race* of the wives (remember Ruth and Rahab). The issue was the *abominations* or *detestable practices*. Because the returned exiles were under the legal authority of the Persian empire, the civil penalty required in Old Testament law for such practices was not applied. But this was no reason to keep the church and families from applying it, and, in the book of Ezra, that is what they did.

So while it is true that a Christian is not supposed to divorce his non-Christian spouse, this only applies if the non-Christian is willing to be married within God's boundaries. But if the non-Christian is guilty of gross offenses (offenses that carried the death penalty in the light of biblical law), then the Christian should recognize *what has already happened.*

Until the church recognizes this, we will continue to have a stand on divorce that is an exegetical and theological embarrassment. As things now stand, many groups would allow divorce for adultery, but would forbid it if the guilty spouse was a mass murderer. This ethical myopia is the result of studying the passages on divorce in isolation (except for Ezra). In contrast to this, *all* of Scripture should be brought to bear on the subject.

Marriage is not an absolute. It is sanctified because the Word of God has sanctified it. It cannot therefore be made into a vehicle to set aside the Word of God. Many Christians have tolerated evil things simply because they think marriage vows require it. They do not. Marriage vows require us to set aside our self-centeredness. Husbands must love their wives, and wives must respect their husbands. We must set aside our own self-centeredness, *not the Word of God*.

Not I, But the Lord

In 1 Corinthians 7:10–11, Paul says, "Now to the married I command, yet not I but the Lord: A wife is not to depart from her husband. But even if she does depart, let her remain unmarried or be reconciled to her husband. And a husband is not to divorce his wife."

The key to understanding this passage is the parenthetical phrase "not I but the Lord." This does not mean, as some have thought, that Paul is claiming that this teaching is inspired, and the passage that follows in verse 12 (I not the Lord") is uninspired.

It means that Jesus (during his earthly ministry) taught directly on divorce, and Paul is applying his teaching here. Divorce is forbidden, and if it occurs, *someone* is in sin. What God has put together, man does not have the right to separate. This means that divorce cannot be justified "for any and every reason." The Word of God must regulate our behavior in every respect.

But Jesus' teaching, while *foundational*, did not cover every possible situation. This was particularly obvious as the Christian church moved out in the Gentile pagan world, making significant progress. "I didn't want a divorce, but now he has left me. . . ." So Paul goes on and teaches how a Christian is to react in such a situation when the one leaving is an unbeliever.

Sin in the realm of the marriage covenant causes not

only heartache but also much theological controversy. The problem is the legitimacy of remarriage. Most Christian teachers would not insist that you have to live with someone who will not let you live with them. But some would still say that the wronged person does not have the right to remarry. This is like saying that stealing is wrong, but that if someone steals your stereo, make sure you don't buy another one. This overlooks the fact that *the thief* is the one who is committing the sin. Violators of the marriage covenant are always in sin. But the weight of this should fall on the one guilty of the violation, not the person sinned against.

We see, then, that sin which leads to divorce is prohibited, with *no* exceptions. Violators of the covenant are always in sin, *and it is the violator of the covenant who is the cause of the divorce.* But the Bible teaches that it is legitimate for us to recognize what the violators of the covenant have done. It is also legitimate for the spouse who was sinned against to recognize the status of the offender.

So, if the divorce *paperwork* is a godly recognition of the other person's rebellion against God, then it is not rebellion against God. But if a divorce is initiated without any basis in the Word of God, then that divorce is sin. In order to be righteous, the divorce must be *responsive*— responsive to God, and to God's assessment of the sin of the spouse.

The fact that conservative Bible teachers differ with this does not mean that this is a liberal view of divorce. There are two ways to tamper with the Word of God. One is to add to the Bible's teaching, and the other is to subtract from it. There are many well-meaning Christians who have set standards on this subject that are stricter than those of the Bible. And it is not truly conservative to be stricter than God.

But what about those who, by the time they read this book, have already done everything wrong? They are now on their third marriage and are troubled with guilt. The good news is that God picks us up where we are, not where we should have been. There is always forgiveness in Christ. Those in such a situation should confess the sin, accept God's forgiveness by faith, *and begin to live in submission to the Word of God.*

Epilogue

Our culture is characterized by men who are embarrassed to be *men*. We have, in our folly, wandered from the Bible's teaching on masculinity, and its central importance for Christian homes. We have sought, with all the wisdom of foolish men, to replace the hardness of masculinity with the tenderness of women. The results in our marriages and families—and consequently for our culture—have been nothing short of disastrous.

Men are bewildered with the world around them and with the responsibilities that a man of God should bear in such a world. Some meekly submit to our cultural rebellion against masculinity; others silently fume, not knowing what to do; others pay lip-service to the concept of equality as a means of exercising ungodly power over women; still others settle for the scraps and remnants they are tossed. *They* do not think they have given up their masculinity, all because they consume a considerable amount of time with sports, cars, and tractor pulls. But masculinity must be genuine, and it must be poured into the *home*.

The castration of Christian men, and the consequent feminization of the family, church, and culture, began in earnest in the last century when the power of an efficacious gospel of grace was abandoned, and the substitute of religious sentiment was set up instead. In our doctrinal defiance, the feminine response of faith was confused with the masculine initiative of God in the gospel. Husbands, who are required in Scripture to imitate the love of Christ, were then taught the error that the love of Christ for His people was impotent. The *efficacy of love* was then abandoned, and the *sentiment of loving* was enthroned. And men became impotent in their imitation of an impotent Lord.

On the cross, Christ conquered sin and death, and ransomed a people to be called by His name. In short, the cross was efficacious, and the evangelical church used to bear consistent testimony to that truth. When the gospel is understood, and husbands are exhorted to imitate Christ in His love for the church in their love for their wives, they undertake the imitation of an efficacious love. But in the last century, the church slowly drifted away from this scriptural understanding of the cross. The power of the cross to save sinners began to be denied, but for evangelicals the cross still had to mean *something*. And as a result the church began to emphasize the sentiment of Christ's loving instead of the efficacy of Christ's love. Softly and tenderly Jesus was calling, and evangelicals, *en masse*, began to leave home.

As a result, men, when they were now exhorted to imitate Christ's love for the church, had nothing but this erroneous teaching about Christ's love to imitate. The ruinous results are all around us. One who has a lump in his throat may not be experiencing the power of God, but he still feels *something* going on. It may be years before he discovers the fraud. The years have passed in our culture, and we have discovered that the fruit is indeed bitter—adultery, disrespectful wives, harsh husbands, divorce, rebellious children, abortion, sodomy. Still, we have not yet come to understand that the bitter fruit comes from a tree that we planted.

We must recognize and acknowledge that our culture's current revolt against the Most High was one that *began* in the families of the church, among those who professed the Lord's name. Salt that loses its savor is trampled by men. Husbands who do not imitate the efficacious love of Christ will see their families trampled as well. Over the last century, this is precisely what we have seen.

As we pray for the reformation of marriage, we must pray that the Christian husband comes to renew or make some basic covenantal commitments before the Lord.

He must first decide that he will thoroughly acquaint himself with the Bible's teaching on marriage, headship, and the family, and that he will gladly submit to it, and put it into practice in his home. He will find himself able to say with understanding, for the first time, "as for me and my house, we will serve the Lord."

He will love His wife as Christ loved the church, giving himself up for her. He will assume the responsibility for her loveliness.

He will not place any responsibility for the spiritual, emotional, physical, and financial condition of his household on his parents, wife, children, church, or society. He will assume, before the Lord, all responsibility for the home he represents before God, and he will pray for the grace to stand.

He will not allow his children to be taught, educated, or raised by men and women who live and teach in rebellion against God. He will remove his children from the government schools and educate them at home or in a godly school.

He will not take his wife away from her primary duties as a mother and manager of the home. He will bring her home to the children, the place God ordained for her to be, and he will encourage and love her in that vocation. He will establish her in the place where she can attain greatness, and when she has attained it, he will rise up and call her blessed.

He will not mistake the love for his wife that God requires of him with the counterfeit "niceness" that abdicates his responsibility for leadership.

He will teach his wife the Word of God, and together they will teach their children.

He will work hard so that his wife is able to clothe and feed the family.

He will be devoted to his wife sexually, treating her with understanding and wisdom.

He will set the tone of his home through his patience, reverence, dignity, kindness, and courtesy.

And he will thank God for His mercy, through the Lord Jesus Christ.